D1507310

Your Emerging Leadership Journey

How to be promoted to a leadership position in less than 10 years

JOHN H. KING, JR.
AND
DR. RONALD F. CICHY

iUniverse, Inc.
New York   Bloomington

Your Emerging Leadership Journey
How to be promoted to a leadership position in less than 10 years

Copyright © 2010 by John H. King, Jr. and Dr. Ronald F. Cichy

All rights reserved. No part of this book may be used or reproduced by any means, graphic, electronic, or mechanical, including photocopying, recording, taping or by any information storage retrieval system without the written permission of the publisher except in the case of brief quotations embodied in critical articles and reviews.

The views expressed in this work are solely those of the author and do not necessarily reflect the views of the publisher, and the publisher hereby disclaims any responsibility for them.

iUniverse books may be ordered through booksellers or by contacting:

iUniverse
1663 Liberty Drive
Bloomington, IN 47403
www.iuniverse.com
1-800-Authors (1-800-288-4677)

Because of the dynamic nature of the Internet, any Web addresses or links contained in this book may have changed since publication and may no longer be valid.

ISBN: 978-1-4401-7194-9 (sc)
ISBN: 978-1-4401-7195-6 (ebk)

Printed in the United States of America

iUniverse rev. date: 12/16/2009

DEDICATION

This work is dedicated to all the leaders who have served as trusted mentors, role models, and valued guides for us in our personal and professional leadership journeys.

CONTENTS

PREFACE

We wrote this book after testing the concepts of Emerging Leadership in our senior-level elective course in Emerging Leadership at Michigan State University. We have team-taught this course since 2006, and, frankly, students have told us how needed this topic is in their hospitality business curriculum. In addition, emerging leaders in service industries who have attended our executive development programs have said that they are using these concepts in their own personal and career leadership journeys. We thank our students for their honest and forthright feedback and we look forward to observing their emerging leadership in their careers.

John H. King, Jr.
Northville, Michigan

Ronald F. Cichy, PhD, NCE5, CHA Emeritus, CFBE, CHE
Okemos, Michigan

ABOUT THE AUTHORS

John H. King, Jr. and his team embarked on their quality journey in 1991. He is the retired president and chief executive officer of HDS Services, a national management and consulting services company. He had been with the company for more than four decades, holding various positions including food services manager, corporate director of operations, vice president (his first leadership position at age 33), executive vice president, and president since 1975. He earned a BS degree in premed from Washington and Jefferson College and attended Michigan State University for one year to obtain a business degree.

Since 1994, King has been a visiting industry professor for senior-level and graduate students in *The* School of Hospitality Business, an industry-specific school within the Eli Broad College of Business and the Eli Broad Graduate School of Management at Michigan State University. In May 1995, he was honored with the Richard J. Lewis Quality of Excellence Award from the Eli Broad College of Business at Michigan State University for his team-taught innovative course in Total Quality Management, a course he developed for over a decade in business and his classroom.

King was a member of the Board of Directors of HDS Services. He also chaired the company's Operating Committee, which drove most of the company's activity. King chaired the Senior Quality Improvement Team as well, and he served on the Executive Committee of the corporate alliance between HDS Services and HHA Services, a plant operations/environmental services organization specializing in health care. King has been a speaker on the topic of managing and improving quality for executives of several organizations, including HHA Services and the Michigan Association of Homes and Services for the Aging (MAHSA).

King continues to support the Managing for Quality course as a visiting speaker, and, in 2006 developed and began team teaching the Emerging Leadership course in *The* School of Hospitality Business at Michigan State University.

Dr. Ronald F. Cichy is the director and a professor in *The* School of Hospitality Business at Michigan State University, a position in which he has served at his alma mater since 1988. He was promoted to his initial leadership position at the age of 24 as the general manager of a resort hotel. Cichy is a frequent speaker at annual conferences, meetings, and institutes for businesses ranging from Fortune 500 companies to the hospitality industry. His topics are both educational and entertaining. His insights come from decades of industry experience and working with top global service leaders. Cichy's work on four continents has developed managers and leaders, team builders and trainers, and helped businesses become high-performance organizations.

His most recent books are *Food Safety: Managing with the HACCP System*, 2nd ed.; *Purchasing for Food Service Operations*, coauthored with Dr. Jeffery D. Elsworth; *Managing Service in Food and Beverage Operations*, 3rd ed., coauthored with Philip J. Hickey, Jr.; and *Managing for Quality in the Hospitality Industry*, coauthored with John King.

Cichy is recognized as a pioneer researcher on leadership qualities, keys, secrets, essentials, and emotional intelligence of hospitality leaders, both in the United States and Japan. His research has led to his identification as one of the most influential scholars in hospitality management.

Cichy serves on the boards of several hospitality industry institutes, foundations, and associations. In 1999, the Educational Institute of the American Hotel and Lodging Association honored Cichy as the Outstanding Hospitality Educator with the Lamp of Knowledge Award. In 2001, Cichy was inducted into *The* School of Hospitality Business Alumni Association's Wall of Fame Class of Contributors. *The* School's Alumni Association honored Cichy as a Distinguished 75th Anniversary Year Alumnus in 2002. The Eli Broad College of Business presented Cichy with its Distinguished Alumnus Award in 2003. Cichy has been recognized by MSU for his scholarly publications in 2004, 2005, 2007, 2008, and 2009. In 2006, Cichy received the Anthony G. Marshall Award, presented by the Educational Institute of the American Hotel & Lodging Association, acknowledging his significant long-term contributions to the hospitality industry in educating future leaders. Cichy was honored with the prestigious Certified Hotel Administrator (CHA) Emeritus by the Educational Institute of the American Hotel & Lodging Association in 2008.

PART I

INTRODUCTION TO LEADERSHIP

CHAPTER ONE—
YOUR LEADERSHIP VISION

"No one is in charge of your happiness, attitude, and career except you."

CHAPTER TWO—
THE LEADERSHIP JOURNEY

"Make peace with your past so it will not spoil the present."

CHAPTER ONE
YOUR LEADERSHIP VISION

YOU WILL EMERGE A LEADER

Here we are in 2009 in the midst of a serious downturn in the country's economy. It is also a period of extended and serious drought in leadership capability. If ever there was a time for those in leadership positions to step forward and change how we lead, *it is now*. Examples of failure are everywhere in today's leadership circles, resulting from greed, arrogance, and the absence of values in corporate executive suites and political arenas. The downsides of this dilemma are obvious. However, there is a more positive angle which involves students and managers who aspire to become leaders. There will be many leadership opportunities as you progress on your career journey.

Your emergence as a leader will occur in a relatively short period of time if you can take the lessons from this book and put them into practice as you proceed on your personal and professional journey.

Our convictions about leadership and learning led us to author this book for two reasons. First we wanted to share our leadership experiences with as many emerging leaders as possible, because we were fortunate to have become leaders at a fairly young age. We did this in spite of not being exposed to any leadership curricula while matriculating in the undergraduate or graduate learning environments. Had we taken a course in leadership, we probably would have been more successful, not to say we did not enjoy success, but rather the success would have been accelerated because there would have been a shorter learning curve.

Secondly, we needed a book to support the students in our Emerging Leadership class. After teaching Managing for Quality for eleven years, we decided to move on to leadership by sharing our experiences in career advancement. We were confident that we could enhance the efforts of students and managers to become leaders at a relatively young age. So, in 2006 we simultaneously embarked on researching and writing this book and launching the leadership class.

Twenty-eight students had committed to take the new Emerging Leadership class at *The* School of Hospitality Business at Michigan State University in the fall of 2006. This was the first time a leadership class had been offered that targeted graduating seniors and focused on how to make the transition from student, through management, and on to leadership in less than ten years. This would seem to most managers and students to be extremely optimistic, and perhaps unrealistic. After all, the majority of undergraduate students perceive the journey as a long-term challenge, with little or no control over the eventual outcome. Our objectives for accelerated career advancement are based on our personal experiences and the experiences of other leaders whom we admire. We know how we achieved our leadership positions, and we want to share the keys to this success with others. The Emerging Leadership class was a new approach and was based on our personal model. Our intent was to teach the students how to assertively succeed in reaching a leadership-level position in an organization through a planned and strongly focused approach. Some managers have been successful, but this has been the exception. At the completion of that first semester's emerging leadership course, our students were actively pursuing career positions and were much better prepared for their initial position assignments and their leadership journeys. We were and are confident that many in the class will achieve their objective of a leadership position within the ten-year time frame. Students who have been successful in accomplishing the transition without this class are very fortunate, but we know many more could duplicate this success if they were thoroughly prepared to do so. There were thirty students in the second leadership class in the fall 2007 semester and an additional thirty in the fall 2008 semester.

At the first class session of each semester, we conducted a brainstorming exercise to determine the students' expectations of the class. Some examples of what they hoped to gain from the class were to learn more about themselves and position themselves to become leaders, make a name for themselves and get their careers off to a good start, apply all of their courses completed so far to their leadership, surround themselves with leaders, build their leadership skills, become more competitive in business, learn how to earn respect rather than simply command authority, learn how to lead people twice their age, and fine-tune their leadership skills. Expectations articulated during the first class also included being an effective leader rather than just a boss, being a more effective communicator, using leadership to improve the skills of associates, learning how to motivate people, rubbing elbows with wise leaders, gaining perspectives on leadership, and setting themselves apart from other leaders.

STUDENT TRANSFORMATION

Near the start of each semester, we asked the students to write us a letter, dated at the end of the semester, detailing why they believed that they deserved an A in the class. This exercise helps them visualize what they are willing to do in the class to earn a top grade. Here are several excerpts from their responses:

- "In addition to completing the required components and earning top marks, I have added countless tools to my arsenal of leadership metaphors, action plans, schools of thought, and shared them accordingly. I feel I will be an ambassador of young leadership within *The* School of Hospitality Business."

- "I achieved my goal of learning about my own values and was able to find a position which fit my objectives and career path. This has been a great experience, as I have been able to venture into myself and find out who I really am."

- "This class has brought about a passion and inspiration in me that I never before experienced in a classroom setting. Thank you."

- "This class and the work and lessons learned help in building me as a person and as a student. I have not done work with this type of learning experience ever in any class."

- "I truly value the lessons in wisdom conveyed to me in this class. We are not required to take notes, but I did because I knew it would be useful information throughout my life."

- "This class is a whole different dynamic because it revolves around teaching young leaders to be the best that they can be in the real world. It is not going to matter a year from now what grade you got, but rather if you are utilizing/practicing the skills you learned from this course. A grade is just a letter that is rather insignificant in the grand scheme of things."

- "I have developed as an individual, and become the person I wanted to be. This course was structured in a way that my answers were not right or wrong. One day I want to be a powerful leader, and, thanks to this course, I have already begun my transformation into that position."

- "I gained valuable leadership and communication skills through active participation in class. I learned a lot about who I am and how to inspire peers and colleagues in a mutually respectful way."

- "I particularly liked the brainstorming activities we experienced as self-directed teams. They taught me the importance of listening to other people's opinions and ideas."

- "Most importantly, I was also able to gain ideas and thoughts from thirty other classmates, as well as two knowledgeable professors, who are all in the hospitality network and passionate about the same things I am."

These statements have been very inspirational and enlightening to us as professors and authors. They used the term "transformation of self," referring to themselves as totally different individuals at the conclusion of the semester. It was clear to us that they had begun to change dramatically during the three and a half months of the class. The metamorphosis had started. They were much more mature; they now look at the management and leadership opportunities with more understanding and willingness to start the journey.

Basically, there are three sets of traits and skills that all great managers and leaders must possess. These are emotional intelligence (people skills), business acumen, and personal values. Leaders see the organization much differently than managers. Managers see the tasks at hand while leaders see the organization in its broadest context. Believe it or not, these three sets of traits and skills are largely in place in many people when they reach their midtwenties. Many in-depth discussions took place during class, and, as the semester progressed, they became more confident and at ease when challenging the professors and their own views. Their communication skills developed by leaps and bounds, which enhanced their confidence in their own abilities to state their own points of view. This was clearly manifested in their success with the interviewing process with many interested hospitality organizations.

What Makes Leaders Different?

Leadership examples point to some common themes. They reveal that many of the successful "leadership stars" were simply in the right place at the right time as they progressed up the corporate ladder. The truth of the matter is these individuals possessed an unusual number of management skills, understood the differences between management and leadership, and had a clear vision of what they wanted to be doing at their five- and ten-year career intervals. Typically, management involves learning task-oriented skills, while leadership entails more global responsibilities such as organizational culture development, large-scale changes, and inspiring the associates in an organization toward their vision. Until now, educators, corporate mentors, and consultants have concentrated on management skills including quality, customer focus, idea and feedback generation, developing partnerships, empowerment, and alignment of personal and organizational values, visions, and missions. This has been one of the contributing factors that led to the current shortage of leaders. We need to counter this challenge, and hopefully our leadership book and curriculum will serve to develop many new aspiring leaders.

A PERFECT LEADERSHIP JOURNEY

Rob was a recent college graduate with six months experience in a management position. When celebrating the holidays with family at home in the Midwest, he and several friends decided to pick up and move to the west coast. They had no idea where they would wind up and, particularly, what job opportunities there would be out west. They did know that Michigan was not their first choice for the long run. Weather was definitely a factor.

They reached the west coast the first week in January and settled south of Los Angeles. Rob found a management position within a week. It was similar to his first management position except that it was one step up the ladder. He was now going to be a department head in a sizeable health-care facility. It was not exactly what he was looking for, but it was in the hospitality industry where his interests were. He was in this position for a little less than a year when he received a telephone call from a large national food distributor. The organization's executive team had observed his management potential and was interested in continuing his management journey as part of their sales team. He accepted the sales position, and his performance was exceptional. After five years in sales he was promoted to his first leadership position, regional manager, at the age of twenty-nine. He was subsequently promoted twice, but the important point was his promotion to a leadership position eight years following graduation. This happened because he knew he wanted a leadership position in sales, was willing to work very hard, and had a plan.

Also, there were many distinctive leadership qualities he possessed, which he instinctively used in every step of the short career journey. In addition to being an excellent communicator, he lived his vision every day. Because he felt so strongly about where he wanted to be, he was passionate, confident, and respected by his team, primarily because of his ability to help others.

Now, ten years later, Rob has formed his own company and reached the goal of most who would like to be entrepreneurs. He is now able to apply all of his leadership capabilities to his own organization and reap the financial rewards. This is not to conclude that he has completed the learning cycle of his leadership journey. In a recent conversation, we discussed the extent of what he believes lies ahead in the world of learning.

Rob's initial career vision was for a period of ten years. Now, his vision for himself, his team, and his company has a time frame that will take him to his retirement years.

In our experience, most great leaders are not superheroes. They possess a few outstanding and obvious strengths that they use to achieve results. They also balance their roles and responsibilities across many areas of responsibility and leadership competencies. Rather than devoting time and great effort in only correcting weaknesses, these leaders build on associates' strengths. Jim Trinka wrote, "Good has become the enemy of excellence, because good managers and leaders do not have the time to become great, and that good is good enough." We do not agree.

Again, you do not have to be a superhero to be considered a great leader. You only need to possess about five profound strengths, and those will create a "halo effect" that overshadows perceived weaknesses. Rob's success is the exception and far from the norm. Most young aspiring graduates will encounter barriers in the corporate world that prevent them from becoming leaders at a young age. The most common barrier is the paradigm of the relationship between experience and advancement in the organization.

> Personally, I was fortunate to have worked for a company that was willing to place associates in leadership positions based primarily on ability. I was merely twenty-six years old when assigned to a client facility as a department manager and twenty-nine when promoted to a much larger facility. That was the last pure management-level position I held in my career, because two years later the company placed me in a leadership position. Seven years later they moved me into the position of president. Like Rob's company, our organization's leadership was the exception to the norm, because the age of the candidate for any position was not a major factor. This decision was made by the board of directors and was based on factors such as present respect and trust among management associates, integrity, customer loyalties, vision, a passion for the company's success, skills and attitude, and character.
>
> Now, after forty-one years with HDS Services, a managed services organization, I tell my friends, former associates, and students that I wished I knew in 1975 (when promoted to the president's position) what I knew in 1995 (following the major paradigm shift at HDS Services to the managing for quality principles of management and leadership). If that had been the case, we and the company would have grown at a much faster pace, both in terms of executive abilities and number of client customers. I am certain you have heard these same words spoken by others when looking back on their careers as leaders. This is another reason we are writing this book. We want you to be well ahead of the learning curve at a relatively young age.

LEADERSHIP AS A JOURNEY

These two examples of achieving leadership positions at a relatively young age merely point out that it can be accomplished, not how to go about getting there. This will be described as we proceed with the process of detailing the leadership journey. If you are soon to be a college graduate, young and in a management position, or a current supervisor or manager seeking to be a leader, you can benefit from learning more about this leadership journey. This is a virtual guide to outline each step toward achieving your dream, if in fact it is a leadership position. We are not talking about the latest management or leadership fad. This is about what works as described by those who have been successful leaders for decades.

John H. King, Jr. and Dr. Ronald F. Cichy

Leadership Is Not a Fad

We opened each class with a Leadership Eye Opener which we quote from Oren Harari on Colin Powell's *American Journey*. The first one is: "Too often people are assumed to be empty chess pieces to be moved around by grand viziers. This explains why so many top managers immerse their calendar time in deal making, restructuring, and the latest management fad. How many immerse themselves in the goal of creating an environment where the best, the brightest, the most creative are attracted, retained, and, most importantly unleashed?" Take note that age, experience, and time with the organization are not mentioned. Like a thoroughbred race, it is not who is in front at the various quarter poles that is important. It is who will eventually win the race and bring the most success to the organization. Recognizing people's potential, encouraging them to develop and seek their leadership positions, and having the courage to give them promotions, regardless of age, are the essentials for assuring leadership succession. How long it takes is entirely up to you. Our students now know themselves at the time of graduation. They are also prepared to know others, and how to build effective, lasting relationships between leadership and their associates.

There are other factors involved in making the right decision in promoting an individual to a leadership position. First of all, no one should move directly from being a student into a leadership position without the essential experience in management. Only when one has mastered the management skills should that individual be considered for a leadership position. These management capabilities will be presented in chapter six.

So, what do leaders do? Basically, they take the organization and its people from one place to another that is closer to the "vision" of the organization. This movement is supported by the relationships between the leader and those who choose to follow. The relationship becomes the foundation on which to build the organization, because it is the people who make the organization successful. The relationships are the enablers of people to achieve excellent results on a consistent basis. The leader has the ability to understand a situation from the points of view of the people, also known as associates.

These associates choose to follow the leader because they share the leader's vision and values, and they have total trust that they are being led to something better and improved. They share the leaders' aspirations and are excited about the possibilities that lie ahead. They form teams that drive change without fear and are recognized for their many wins, regardless of impact. In essence, the leadership and associates create an organizational community.

Leadership is also an in-and-out proposition. The leader exports power and authority, and imports ideas, all without concern or consideration for keeping score in a grand balance of trade. Eventually, the many teams within the organization become a flotilla that takes the organization forward toward the vision and success.

In contrast, when others refer to your organization as the *Queen Mary*, it is not a compliment. Changing direction or turning around the ocean-going ship the *Queen Mary* is no easy task, especially if you are sailing in a sea with small, more agile organizations. Effective leaders of larger organizations have been successful in bringing flexibility, quality, empowerment, speed to market, partnering, and in adding value to their organizations.

ARE LEADERS BORN OR DEVELOPED?

The debate about whether great leaders are born or developed has been resolved for the most part by research. In the article "Born to Run," by Al Senter, it is summed up very succinctly: "Examining the background of established leaders suggests there are a number of contributing factors such as first born or only children who spend much of their time exclusively in adult organization. However, future leaders, regardless of their solitary upbringing, often display an innate ability to empathize with others. This makes them a kind of counselor to whom children turn in times of trouble. Also, oftentimes leadership is granted to those with above average height."

Many experts on leadership believe that about 10 percent have been born with innate leadership abilities. Another 10 percent will never become leaders, however favorable their circumstances. But, the 80 percent of people could, if willing, realize their leadership potential through development and training.

Most successful parents are not aware that they are providing their children with the basic character that forms the foundation of being a great leader. The core traits of leaders are a mirror of the values our parents taught us to be a good person. These core values stay with us throughout our lives, to be practiced in both family and work environments. The most significant variable in the continuum is the difference in the generations. This is best described by evaluating the personality traits of the silent generation versus the baby boomers versus the later generations, especially generation Y. We addressed this issue in our leadership class. The bottom line was that the variances in generational personalities were not a major factor as long as the managerial skills and leadership essentials were in place.

John H. King, Jr. and Dr. Ronald F. Cichy

Preparing for a Leadership Position

So, let us return to the leadership journey and begin at the level of the "student." The undergraduate student who knows exactly what career field they want to pursue has a distinct advantage over those who are less certain. Those who are graduating with a degree in a career field they have chosen will have taken the required and elective courses in their discipline and will have work experience and an internship in that discipline at some organization in their chosen industry. Perhaps some will have experienced a supervisory-level internship. Therefore, it is possible, and even probable in the hospitality business curriculum, that they would possess a strong understanding of the required management skills. In addition, those students who choose to take a leadership class will have a definite advantage because it will clarify and sometimes fine-tune or change their personal and career visions. These students will have a very clear picture of how to successfully begin their leadership journeys. Having the knowledge and confidence without fear will greatly enhance their opportunities over the competition.

There are other items to consider and accomplish before moving on to that first position. An internship allows you to confirm the fit—your interest in and level of comfort with your industry of choice. You should evaluate all of the organizations in your chosen field and make sure you select the best organization that meets your expectations. The due diligence process will include size, geography, culture, and history of career development. It is important to realize that there are more traditional organizations out there than there are high-performance organizations. Traditional organizations continue to use the "top down" paradigm and only promote individuals with the appropriate seniority in the organization and the most experience, regardless of leadership potential. Conversely, high-performance organizations use a "bottom up" leadership approach and an individual's potential as a major factor when promoting a candidate. They always choose the best candidates in the selection process, focus on retention, effectively mentor, and empower. If possible, try to meet your first boss and identify possible mentors in the organization during the interviewing process. Look at it this way. You cannot pick your family, but you can pick your future organization and boss.

As a graduating college student, the basic skills, book knowledge, and practical experience include such things as procurement, technology (communications and data), human resources, operations, strategic planning, accounting and finance, business law, sales and marketing, and managing for quality. Obviously, the skills and knowledge required of a student are quite basic compared to those in management and leadership positions. If the graduate has had the opportunity to take a leadership course, the individual will understand the differences between management and leadership.

Another important factor that will influence the success of getting started with a career journey is the understanding of the student's emotional intelligence. Is the individual really ready to move on and leave the formal educational environment behind? Is the person socially mature enough to seriously accept the responsibilities of the first career position and to have well-thought-out aspirations? After all, the college years provide not only for educational advancement but for social and emotional maturation as well. It is important that the career candidate get started on the right foot immediately. The person must be passionate and excited about the first career step, but the individual must also be mature, know what to expect and want, and be very organized in both work and personal life.

Abraham Lincoln's political resume was meager, his learning derided, and his election considered a stroke of luck. As it turned out, he was a political genius because he possessed remarkable emotional strengths (first-class emotional intelligence). The eight examples of his strengths were empathy, humor, magnanimity, generosity of spirit, perspective, self-control, sense of balance, and social conscience. For over a century and in poll after poll, he has been recognized as the "best" American president.

LEADERSHIP LESSON FROM THE EAGLE

Throughout the book, we will be presenting "Leadership Lessons from the Eagle," as we have done in class. The Eagle metaphor is easily understood because of its representation and connectivity to the leadership model. Eagles are our metaphor for leaders. One such lesson is applicable to the beginning phase of one's career, that is, "The flip side of leadership and one's mentoring responsibilities is the high visibility of the leader, and what associates expect from their leader. Fortunately, they are looking for a learning environment, so use this as a strategic advantage." The Eagle will be our role model and mentor as we look for ways to become more effective leaders.

According to Tim Elmore, there is a crying need in our world today for more and better leaders. Why are they rare? Again, for decades, business schools have been forced to concentrate on managerial development, because of the many changes fast-paced growth required in the business world. The goal was to harness others, not explore their potential. Thus, the bureaucracy took over and often stifled progress and possibilities.

Remember the manners your parents taught you, and use them in the position search process, position acceptance, and every day in your relationships with peers, associates, external customers, and others. Financial responsibilities will suddenly be staring you in the face as income becomes a reality. The list of things to do will include setting goals, managing your student loans and paying them back, saving some of your income consistently, including some insurance in your expenses, using frugal habits in spending, checking your credit report, and always reading the fine print before signing any agreement.

Secondly, when the baby boomers were growing up, the world was in turmoil and college campuses were filled with demonstrations against the establishment and businesses, in particular. Students mistrusted the establishment, often called the military-industrial complex, and any semblance of leadership. So, when it was time to learn about leadership, they checked out. Some of the executives in organizations today lacked integrity and ethics. These former executives now find themselves in prison. The last reason is the total lack of focus on succession planning in many organizations. Present leadership must have their eyes on who best will succeed them when it is their time to move on from the organization. Oftentimes the best candidate for a leadership position is not closest to the top.

We suggest that the best candidate is the person with the most leadership potential, regardless of age. That individual should be considered for succession to a leadership position. So, with the shortage of leaders today, you will find abundant opportunities at the leadership level. Conversely, there are many challenges facing leaders today, such as 24 hours a day, seven days a week, and 365 days a year consumer demands; terrorism; jittery markets and consumers; downsizing; fickle customers; a global economy; social capital; financial capital pressure; a "speed"—faster, better, cheaper—culture; and shrinking accountability. Globalization could be one of the most important challenges today, because of the importance of managing cross-culturally. This includes diversity in national cultures as well as internal corporate culture differences between an organization's headquarters and regional offices.

Colin Powell, in his book *My American Journey*, suggested that "organizational planning and management theories are not the most important keys to leadership success. Only by attracting the best people will you accomplish great deeds."

Few, if any, leaders have been successful when surrounded by incompetence. Most successful leaders attribute their accomplishments to the talents of those individuals on their team. In other words, the leader is not the driving force behind success. The skills, capabilities, competencies, and dedication of the people who work with the leader are directly responsible for success.

In addition, the leader must be open to criticism and suggestions from the team because the day associates stop bringing the leader their issues or suggestions is the day you have stopped leading them. When associates ask for help, it is not a display of weakness. It is more a sign of confidence in your leadership.

In contrast to the previously described leader/team relationship, there will occasionally be a situation in which being a responsible leader will make associates angry. This will involve making a decision for the good of the team at the expense of an associate. If leaders want all associates to like them, they will only achieve mediocrity, or at best win a popularity contest. Popularity is not leadership; achieving the desired results for the individuals and the organization is a critical dimension of effective leadership.

With the lack of adequate numbers of leaders, the business world is forced to accept younger leaders. Are you ready to "take the wheel"?

> This statement has particular significance to me. I clearly remember these words spoken to me at a very young age. I was sixteen or seventeen years old when my father informed me that I would be starting driver's training the morning of the next day. The initial reaction was "yeah." However, I was not sure what to expect because I had never been behind the wheel of an automobile. Being a young man who had overcome many learning obstacles in the past, the apprehension was gone in minutes. The next day, the instructor and the car arrived right on time. After a two-minute introduction to this compact car and how it operated, including the stick shift, the instructor demonstrated how it worked by driving around the block and stopping exactly where we had started the demonstration, on the street in front of our home.
>
> This was not your typical subdivision street. It was a four-lane highway that connected the west and east coasts of the United States. It was U.S. Route 30, better known as the Lincoln Highway. The instructor looked me in the eye and said: "Take the wheel, John." I remember being scared to death as trucks and cars raced past this compact car parked in the right lane of the highway. We switched seats and I immediately became a driver for the first time. Like most people I had difficulty with the clutch and accelerator, and must have stalled the car five times as the passing vehicles honked their horns at me. I do remember taking this humiliation personally, but within minutes I was moving and looking for the first street to escape from the highway. Many years later I still "take the wheel" everyday, but with a much different attitude than that first time.

When you meet your associates for the first time in your first management position, you will be asked to "take the wheel."

In an interview in the fall of 2006 with *Forbes Magazine*, Peter Drucker, one of the world's most famous leadership sages, and 95 years of age, was asked for his thoughts on leadership. The following are the observations he made:

1. Do not be afraid of strength in others. Surround yourself with the best talent available, hopefully more able than you.

2. Check your performance at least every six months. Rate yourself against your goals, and make sure you are doing the right things.

3. There will continue to be pressure on leaders to accomplish many things at once, so be prepared to say no and stick with it.

4. Know when to stop pouring resources into a project. Lead change and do not fear creative abandonment.

5. Concentrate on building your strengths.

6. Organize your company around clients rather than localities. Internet meetings are changing how we meet.

7. Be sure your associates understand your priorities.

8. Do not try to be someone else.

We will begin now to set the stage for your future by covering the journey to becoming a leader in your chosen industry.

CHAPTER ONE

REFERENCES

Elmore, Tim. "That Sucking Sound You Hear." The Leadership Link Growing Leaders, Inc., September 2006. Retrieved on May 9, 2009, from www. Growingleaders.com Web site: http://growingleaders.com/images/stories/is%20sucking%20a%20leader.pdf

Harari, Oren. *The Leadership Secrets of Colin Powell.* New York: McGraw Hill, 2002.

Karlgaard, Rich. "Peter Drucker on Leadership." Interview with Forbes.com, November 19, 2004. Retrieved on May 9, 2009, from www.Forbes.com Web site: http://www.forbes.com/2004/11/19/cz_rk_1119drucker_print.html

Powell, Colin L. and Joseph E. Persico. *My American Journey.* New York: Ballantine Books, August 1996.

Senter, Al. "Born to Run." *Director*, January 2002, 55 (6): 40–42.

Trinka, Jim. "Great Leaders." *Leadership Excellence*, July 2005, 22 (7): 17.

Chapter Two
The Leadership Journey

The Journey: Where Are You Now? Where Are You Going?

Your personal leadership journey has already started. It began in your student learning years and was expanded in your role as a manager. In this chapter, you are encouraged to evaluate where you are in your journey in light of the leadership qualities, keys, and secrets. As we suggested that you align your personal management goals with those of the organization, you will need to tie your personal leadership journey to that of your organization. When the two journeys are aligned, achievement will have no boundaries. Alignment will result in involvement with senior management, and it will give you the opportunity to display your potential through presenting your views on where the organization is, where it is going, and positive suggestions on how to get there.

All of the best leaders recognize that the journey never ends, because developing and executing change will go on forever. If you never give up, continuous improvement on both the personal and organization fronts will remain your priority. In an earlier time, Elbert Hubbard, an American writer, stated: "The line between failure and success is so fine that we are often on the line and do not know it. How many a man has thrown up his hands at a time when a little more effort and patience would be achieved success. A little more effort and what seemed hopeless failure may turn to glorious success." Hubbard is obviously referring to both women *and* men as they act on opportunities in their leadership journeys.

John H. King, Jr. and Dr. Ronald F. Cichy

Personal Leadership Qualities

We have discussed some of the leadership qualities you probably possessed as a student and a manager. Your organization's executive staff continually evaluates your leadership potential throughout your career based on the presence or lack of these qualities. Generally speaking, these could include integrity, communication, mentoring, decision making, and empowering. We will discuss these in more detail later. The first step in the journey involves knowing yourself and your capabilities. Do you possess some of these qualities? What will you need to learn before going forward into the role of leadership?

The secrets of effective leadership relate to your personality and how you will lead. There are several personal traits necessary to complement your leadership qualities and keys in order for you to be an effective leader. Associates want their leaders to be confident, accountable, responsible, and dependable, to name a few. Again, the secrets relate to the leader's personal traits and character.

The leadership keys relate to methods of leading that are important to associates. They include trust in associates, expertise, envisioning the future, and a calm/cool demeanor.

Qualities, Keys, and Secrets of Effective Leadership

As discussed earlier in this book and reinforced now, sooner rather than later you must be aware of the qualities, keys, and secrets of being an effective leader and practice these each day. Your daily practice ensures that you will be prepared for your managerial career as well. You want to be noticed during the managerial stage of your career, and having knowledge of the qualities, keys, and secrets will serve to strengthen your quest for attaining a leadership position. Practicing these will get you noticed and will accelerate the timing of managerial promotions. Your associates will be the first to notice your attributes and potential, so be a servant leader. This means putting the interests, needs, and aspirations of associates ahead of yours. Be other-centered rather than self-centered.

The qualities, keys, and secrets were originally identified in the 1980s through classic leadership studies by scholars Bennis and Nanus (1985); Roberts (1985), who studied a popular approach to business leadership; and also by Labach (1988), who studied an unusual treatment of business leadership. In 2003, Cichy, Cha, and Knutson researched the underlying dimensions of private club leadership using the essentials identified in the previous studies of the 1980s. Data for the more recent study were aggregated from 1996 to 2003 using 702 participants identified as chief operating officers or general managers who were members of the Club Managers Association of America (CMAA) and attendees of the Business Management Institute (BMI III) at Michigan State University.

The participants were asked to rank qualities, keys, and secrets in order of importance for being an effective leader. Remember, the qualities are what you use to lead, the keys are methods of leadership, and the secrets are related to your personality and how you will lead.

The top three qualities were:

- Recognize that the ability to adjust is a necessity.
- Provide a compelling message or vision.
- Have a strong personal value or belief system.

The top three keys were:

- Trust your people.
- Develop a vision.
- Keep your cool.

The top three secrets were:

- Dependability
- Credibility
- Self-confidence

Leadership Qualities

1. **Recognize the ability to adjust is a necessity.**
   This addresses the importance of leadership's ability to guide the organization, its customers, and its associates through change. Change leads to continuous improvement, which leads to maintaining or enhancing organizational growth, and ultimately leads to the survival of the organization. The leader is the facilitator of changing processes within the organization. As a manager you learn how to create change; as a leader you bring the associates together to achieve complete commitment to change. You will generate more ideas for change when the diversity within your teams is increased. Effective leaders listen to their associates because they are the source of most of the great ideas that create positive change.

> At HDS Services, the associates generated one thousand ideas over a period of ten years. They were responsible for creating the new culture of managing for quality at HDS Services.

Winston Churchill, the British prime minister during World War II, exemplified an innovative leader because he had a very experimental mind. He said: "No idea is outlandish that it should not be considered with a searching, but at the same time a steady eye."

2. **Provide a compelling message or vision.**

   While the organization's vision is developed by teams of associates from all levels of the organization, as a leader you will be responsible for taking your entire team toward that end. The leader's personal vision, values, and mission must be aligned with the organization's vision, values, and mission. Every decision made by management and leadership must be aligned with the vision. Effective leaders demonstrate consistency in this area because they are not only committed to the vision, they live it.

3. **Have a strong personal value or belief system.**

   These qualities must include integrity, associate-first orientation, customer-first focus, value of teams, trust, openness, and loyalty. Managers and, more importantly, leaders must regularly check their values compass to ensure their values reflect their belief system. After all, these values are what got you where you are in the first place. Any divergence from these values will create problems for the associates and eventually for the organization as a whole. Leaders with strong personal values should express these values and get as close to key customers as possible. This provides the organization with a strategic advantage.

> At HDS Services, the top three executives personally visited all clients once each year. These high-level meetings were not about customer satisfaction, but to let the customer know where the company was going, that its values were still strong, and to reinforce continuous improvement in the company's culture.

Two additional qualities in the top five are that leaders "listen as well as, if not better than, they speak" and leaders "make desired outcomes tangible." Listening is the most important communication skill. Empathetic listening is practiced when you listen from the other person's point of view. Tangible desired outcomes help others see the results to be achieved and what they can do to contribute.

Leadership Keys

1. **Trust your people.**

   Successful managers and leaders must provide all team members with the ability to plan the work they do in order that they may derive pride and joy in their work. This culture is 100 percent dependent on trust by both associates and the organization's leadership. The most respected and successful organizations, such as Ritz-Carlton, Nordstrom, Disney, and others, empower their associates, which leads to high morale, high performance, more loyal customers, and overall growth.

2. **Develop a vision.**

   As previously mentioned, everyone must know where they personally and the organization are going. A vision answers the question: "What do we want to create in the future?" and serves as a focal point for action. When associates know where the organization is headed, they can commit to the vision, which accelerates success at all levels.

3. **Keep your cool.**

   Many of the issues and challenges that end up on the leader's desk are major and have implications at all levels of the organization. Associates will notice the initial reactions of the leader, and, if not received in a calm, professional manner, there will be possible deterioration of respect for the leader. Associates are looking for answers and direction, not an uncontrolled outburst. Keeping your cool helps the leader and others develop sound and objective solutions.

Two additional keys in the top five are "simplify" and "be an expert." When leaders simplify complex issues, they unlock ways that all in the organization can understand and contribute. Leaders build their management expertise during the early phases of their leadership journeys. Expertise results from being competent as managers and leaders. Leadership built on the foundation of competency is strong and able to withstand the many challenges that leaders and their followers face. Competent leaders are respected by followers.

Leadership Secrets

1. **Dependability**

   Associates depend on leadership to respond to questions, resolve issues, implement change, and recognize achievement. Dependable managers and leaders get things done. They are also there for you when needed and are great mentors. They care and are empathetic. Their words and actions are consistent.

2. Credibility

Credible managers and leaders always do the "right thing" for the individual, team, and organization as a whole. They follow the Golden Rule—do unto others as you wish them to do unto you—which is found in some form in over twenty of the world's religions. These leaders use their strong ethics in the decision-making process. They mean what they say and follow through on **all** commitments. Credibility is the foundation of leadership, because without it the leader is totally ineffective. When the leader embraces the associates' expectations and together those needs are met, there will be credibility. Associates want to work for leaders who are honest, have a vision, and are competent and inspiring. Credibility influences customer, associate, and investor loyalty, and we know that loyalty is responsible for extraordinary value creation. Leaders will always have their credibility questioned by the opposition. So, you must be very vigilant in guarding your credibility. Your ability to take a strong stand, to challenge the status quo, and to help associates see the right direction depends upon the leader being perceived as being highly credible.

The foundation of credibility is character. Noel Tichy and Warren Bennis in their article "Wise Leaders" indicate that "character is that distinctive, unfiltered personal voice that cannot be faked or imitated. It is the core essence of who we are. In today's world, it is more powerful than ever in shaping our actions. You need to ride the breaking wave of change, because there is no stopping along the way to change your equipment." Leaders with good character accept responsibility for their actions and literally hold themselves accountable for the consequences.

3. Self-confidence

Confident leaders more easily and quickly make the right decisions. This is a result of experience, or at least having a strong sense for what is right for the associates and customers. There are three sets of expectations to consider in the decision-making process: associates, customers, and financial. Steven Jobs, CEO and cofounder of Apple, demonstrated credibility by having an open-.door policy. He gave all of his associates his home phone number so they would phone him if they needed anything. He also established credibility by paying himself only one dollar annual salary. He could have paid himself anything he wanted, because he founded the organization, but he chose not to do so.

The other leadership secrets in the top five are "responsibility" and "accountability." Leaders are accountable to their followers, others in the organization, customers, and the owners. Leaders who are accountable carefully choose their actions to move the organization forward. Responsibility is closely linked to accountability. Responsible leaders are role models for others, and they inspire others through their actions.

FIVE ESSENTIALS OF LEADERSHIP

When leadership qualities, keys, and secrets are studied and combined over multiple years, the five essentials of leadership were identified.

Innovation

The first essential was identified as being *innovative*. This is the driving force behind positive change, continuously improving products and services, market share growth, financial stability, and long-term existence. There is no such thing as having too much creativity in the organization. Surround yourself with as many innovators as possible. Albert Einstein once said, "Logic will get you from A to B. Imagination will take you everywhere." Leaders must foster creativity and promote risk taking without fear of failure. There must be a willingness to change your mind and the direction without fear of waffling. These leaders place significant emphasis on learning for everyone. And, lastly, they always surround themselves with people who are not like them, rather those with complementary skills.

Vision

Can innovation force a change in the organization's *vision*, the second essential? Yes, it can alter the vision. That is why the vision must be revisited annually for possible modification due to major change implementation. The organization's vision impacts every decision made within the organization, and it provides a beacon to guide leaders and followers, particularly in turbulent and uncertain times.

Strong Inner Values

The third essential is the possession of *strong inner values*. This starts with family values that pour over into the business. This leader knows his or her own strengths, as well as the strengths of the associates, and nurtures them. Rather than concentrating on the few weaknesses by trying to produce a "perfect associate," a leader takes advantage of the associates' strengths, places them in the most appropriate position, and works toward improving the strengths of their associates. And, the leader should have a good sense of humor to get us all through difficult and trying times. Leaders must tell the truth all the time. They must choose the ethical course of action, while radiating a sense of urgency.

Inspire

The fourth essential is the ability to *inspire* others. Leaders firmly believe there is no such thing as failure, only next steps, because mistakes are, in fact, opportunities. This leadership essential certainly is consistent with those who empower their associates by providing resources, support, and information. Then they get out of the way so the associates can make decisions. These associates know precisely what the true purpose/mission of the organization is and what their individual role is in moving in that direction.

Communicate

The last essential involves the ability to *communicate*. Communications cover many skills, one of which is public speaking. In this scenario there is immediate feedback from your audience, both positive and negative. More important, though, is listening. Good communicators are often more inquisitive and ask the best questions. They also are great listeners, and their associates are well aware of how well this is done. It is essential to practice listening to others each time you are engaged in a conversation. The best communicators know how to listen to themselves. In doing this, they know when to stop talking and start to listen to what others have to say. How many times have you heard someone ramble on and on and repeat themselves multiple times in the same conversation? These people do not listen to themselves, because if they did, they would not repeat themselves. Also, you will notice that these individuals have no interest outside of their own in hearing what the other person has to say.

Dianna Booher, in her article "10 Questions to Stellar Communication," indicates that communication makes the "top three" leadership lists in most instances. Leaders lead change and take responsibility for the communication culture. Managers maintain and go with the status quo. Leaders become the face or human connection of the organization. They connect with other people such as customers, associates, and particularly members of the executive team. They communicate values, and act consistently within those values. In addition, they always tell the truth. They never use "spin," or telling others what they want to hear, even though this has become a part of everyday communication. Also, good leaders admit when they are wrong; thus people believe them when they are right.

Additional Leadership Characteristics and Skills

Additional characteristics of effective leaders include commitment, passion, professionalism, sincerity, positive thinking, courage, and community involvement.

Other skills include mentoring, understanding of technology, street sense, strategic planning, building of relationships, resolving conflicts, and written communication. Courage and commitment are two powerful characteristics. Basically, commitment is the will to never give up. Recognizing there is a difference between being successful and winning is critical in the journey to be the best, world class, or number one. Vince Lombardi, the legendary coach of the Green Bay Packers, once said: "The difference between a successful person and being a winner is not a lack of strength, not a lack of knowledge, but rather a lack of will." Winston Churchill said: "Courage is rightly esteemed as the first human quality, because it is the quality which guarantees all others."

Leaders must possess the courage to take action based on their values, and this results in what is known as good judgment. We are not talking about physical courage here. We are talking about the "emotional or feelings side" of courage that enables the leader to see what is the right way or journey and always take the high road. This high road becomes the hard road at times. Big decisions involve greater risk, but remember that you are in the leadership role because of your good judgment and courage. Whatever the situation may be, always use the talents of those who work with you to get input and ideas before making the decision that affects them.

Never defer to the expedient in the decision-making process. Use your strong moral fiber along with your other values, and put the greater good of the organization ahead of personal gain. Good decisions come from good judgment, which will drive productive results and deliver the results.

The following is a graphic presentation of the young effective leader, using an eagle as the leadership model.

In reviewing Oren Harari's comments on Colin Powell's *My American Journey*, we find and paraphrase some additional characteristics of real leaders.

Real Leaders

Real leaders are always available. They remove the barriers between executives and the organization's associates. They realize that many associates fear that asking for help or advice displays weakness. Conversely, the real leader encourages associate requests, comments, and general dialogue.

Real leaders also display concern for associates' challenges and recognize their efforts. Conversely, associates fear that this level of associate empathy and concern could lead to demand for higher standards. In the best organizations, associates align themselves with the goals of leadership, and they are directly involved in improving standards at the associates/grassroots level. These real leaders create a culture where solving problems and continuous improvement replace blame.

The obvious question here relates to where leadership recruits and selects these unusual associates who literally become enrolled as advocates. This highlights the importance of an effective, aligned human resources group within the organization. They do not hire candidates; they select them. When selecting the right candidates, they look for intelligence, judgment, capacity to anticipate, loyalty, integrity, high energy, balanced ego, and the drive to get things done. This is only the beginning, because their orientation, learning, and mentoring processes further develop managers and leaders and are equally critical. In addition, everyone, including leadership, is involved in the learning process. Learning organizations have the potential to become known as "world class."

World-Class Organizations

These organizations are not only leaders in their industry; they are acclaimed to be the best. World-class organizations manage for quality and possess this strong commitment for associate/leadership learning and development.

World-class organizations are better prepared to face the multifaceted challenges present in today's environment. These would include massive downsizing efforts, jittery markets, diversified consumer demands, uncertainty, a shrinking magnitude of the globe due to technology, threats of technological forces to diminish face-to-face customer relations, the transitioning of physical capital toward intellectual capital, and uniting an adverse world through global understanding. Shannon Cranford and Sarah Glover in their article "The Stakes Grow Higher for Global Leaders" indicate that challenges for global leaders are vitally important for two reasons: power and complexity. Multinational organizations have enormous power because their influence and impact shape the world socially, economically, and environmentally. There is a major difference between leadership at the local level and that at the global level. The level of complexity grows exponentially at the global level in dealing with managing action, information, people, and pressure, in general. Global leaders deal with managing the relationships between corporate headquarters and local offices, understanding and managing external forces, handling cultural conflicts, adapting personal behaviors, creating shared goals, and communicating across barriers.

These challenges were rooted toward the end of the twentieth century and are now growing. They are complex, without easy answers, but there are several keys to positive response and direction. Reconsider your priorities and put family first, with work second. Be a collaborative leader who puts people first and profits second. Rebuild a sense of community and increase understanding among diverse people. Turn information into knowledge and create a sense of meaning with your team. Create unprecedented values for your customers by applying this knowledge to products and services and the experiences that are created and delivered. When everything is so unpredictable, continue to articulate your vision and mission, and assure that your values continue to drive your actions.

Self-Assessment

Before closing this chapter, it is appropriate to complete a baseline assessment of what you do or do not understand about leadership and where you are in the journey when compared to the management principles, qualities, keys, and secrets. You are asked to quantify your understanding of each of the items in the Balanced Scorecard. Use the following scale of understanding levels rated from five to one.

Leadership Balanced Scorecard

5	4	3	2	1
Totally Understand	Almost There	Moderately Understand	Somewhat Understand	Do Not Understand

Be a Model for Others

Item	Score
Identify your own values, vision, and mission	
Focus on customers and build loyalty	
Share your values, vision, and mission with others	
Practice ethical behavior	
Build consensus	
Set the example	
Align values and actions	
Align personal and organization values	
Gain experience with the responsibilities of your associates	
Create your legacy	
Practice quality of life	

Help Others Become Motivated

Item	Score
Get to know each person	
Establish market leadership / Create a strategic advantage	
Use imagination	
Promote the vision	
Enlist others	
Share the vision	
Promote common values (pay attention)	
Be the vision	
Live the vision	
Coach others in the vision	

Challenge the Way It Is

Item	Score
Innovate	
Encourage others' ideas (most ideas come from followers)	
Emphasize the continuous improvement process	
Identify opportunities	
Identify solutions	
Identify barriers/paradigms that hinder others	
Take action	
Measure progress	
Take risks	
Use failures to learn	
Encourage team initiative	

Enable People

Item	Score
Promote teamwork	
Build teams	
Plan strategically	
Encourage cooperative goal setting	
Measure results	
Empowerment	
Build/earn trust	
Use the power of learning	

Juice People Up

Item	Score
Recognize achievement	
Give constant feedback	
Celebrate successes	
Be a positive influence	

Have fun	
Recognize milestones	

Chapter Two

References

Booher, Dianna. "10 Questions to Stellar Communication." *Leader to Leader,* Fall 2007, 46:42.

Cichy, Ronald F., Jae Min Cha, and Bonnie Knutson. "The Five Essentials of Private Club Leadership." *Florida International Review,* Fall 2004, 22 (2): 46–58.

Cranford, Shannon, and Sarah Glover. "The Stakes Grow Higher for Global Leaders." *Leadership in Action,* July/August 2007, 27 (3): 9.

Goldsmith, Marshall. "Bad Behavior." *Leadership Excellence,* 2007, 24 (2):16.

Harari, Oren. *The Leadership Secrets of Colin Powell.* New York: McGraw Hill, 2002.

Hodgetts, Richard M., Fred Luthans, and Song M. Lee. "New Paradigm Organizations: From Total Quality to Learning to World-Class." *Organizational Dynamics,* winter 1994, 22:5–19.

Hubbard, Fra Elbert. "Note Book of Elbert Hubbard." USA. Roycrofters, 1927.

Kouzes, James M., and Barry Z. Posner. *The Leadership Challenge.* 4th ed. San Francisco: John Wiley & Sons, 2007.

Langstaffe, Caroline. "Winston Churchill, a Leader from History or an Inspiration for the Future?" *Industrial and Commercial Training*, 2005, 37 (2): 80–83.

Young, Jeffrey S., and William L. Simon. *iCon Steve Jobs*. Hoboken, NJ: John Wiley & Sons, 2005.

Part II

Understanding Leadership

CHAPTER THREE–KNOW YOURSELF

"Do not take yourself so seriously, because no one else does. And, what other people think of you is none of your business."

CHAPTER FOUR–INTEGRITY AND HONESTY

"If you tell the truth, you do not have to remember anything."
Mark Twain

CHAPTER FIVE–KNOW OTHERS

"Life is too short to waste time hating anyone."

CHAPTER THREE
KNOW YOURSELF

YOUR INNER WORLD

Now that you have used the Balanced Scorecard (presented in chapter two) to identify and quantify your level of understanding and knowledge about the qualities, keys, and secrets of the effective leader, it is time to get to know your inner self. In class the students accomplish this by taking two professionally developed assessments of their personality. The results of each of these assessments can be compared with their Balanced Scorecard results, as well as the other assessment. Past experience with using the assessment tools tells us that there will be some differences between who you thought you were and what this latest evaluation indicates. In other words, you will now know things about yourself that were previously untapped or hidden in your inner self.

You now need to evaluate the results of these assessments and determine what personal traits and characteristics require development and experience. By evaluate we mean "looking in" and determining who you are and eventually who you want to be. Looking identifies opportunities for improvement and progress with the journey.

As a leader, you are only authentic when leading associates using the principles and values that matter most to you. So, take the journey into your inner self. Look into the dark and locked places to open up your potential for being an effective emerging leader. You *can* do it!

THE SERVANT LEADER

Observing what has happened to leaders who took advantage of their position to take organizational assets for personal use, you are most likely aware of the importance of integrity in the workplace. You should have a clear understanding of why the Securities and Exchange Commission took the stance in the courtroom that some leaders have set a bad example by pushing associates to use improper accounting methods and not informing shareholders and the SEC of their use. William J. Byron, S.J., in his article "The Tools and Qualities of Effective Management" refers to the importance of an organization having the right "tone at the top." The effective leader takes his or her place at the center of the circle, not the top of the pyramid. This is significant because it demonstrates the role of the servant leader. The leader serves others on the team in a facilitating way to continuously bring about changes that were originally suggested by members of the team. This is what is referred to as the bottom-up culture that fosters creativity and ideas from all people in the organization.

The leader of this "circular" organization serves his or her associates and external customers, as well as the owners of the organization. The servant leader serves first, because leading and managing begin with the natural feeling that we want to serve others. After that, conscious choice brings one to aspire to lead. This servant leader has the ability to see through the eyes of the associates, and, speaking from experience, this leader is dramatically different than the one who believes that the "leader comes first."

According to Dave Dow, adjunct professor in *The* School of Hospitality Business at Michigan State, who made a presentation to the students in the fall 2008 Emerging Leadership class, the servant leader possesses several characteristics that other leaders do not. They are the following:

- Listening
- Empathy
- Walking their talk
- Respect for others
- Treating associates fairly
- Mentoring
- Honesty

In addition, the most effective servant leaders are results oriented, able to make the tough decisions, and are decisive. In order to be a servant leader, you must be humble and very secure in your position. You must also be able to tell your associates, "I am sorry," when you make a mistake that affects them or the organization. Leaders who are not secure do not make good servant leaders because they fear the results of empowering associates, that is, to eventually lose power in their leadership position. Managers with less than adequate self-esteem rarely make great leaders.

This type of manager can, however, change over time with strong coaching from his or her mentor. This confirms the support for leadership development versus innate leadership attributes. So, if you are a manager who has yet to acquire and effectively practice the qualities, keys, and secrets of effective leadership, do not give up. You can easily learn the leadership qualities, keys, and secrets and put them into practice. This is where individual assertiveness and self-motivation come into play, because your boss and others on the organization's leadership team need to know about your evaluation results and progress. This is where the potential of managers becomes critical to their success in achieving a position in leadership. When you learn that your Balanced Scorecard and other assessment results do not match or you need to further develop your qualities, keys, and secrets, do not fret or panic. Gaining knowledge about leadership is a developmental journey. Your student journey consumed several years and your management journey will require a minimum of several years more, most likely five to ten.

In addition to developing management and leadership essentials, you must also make certain that the organization in which you are working is the organization you will want to lead in the future. If there are only several minor cultural or leadership challenges with the existing organization, it should not be enough of an issue to drive a career change. Why not? Mainly because once you become part of the leadership team, you will be in a position to make or help drive changes that will resolve your personal issues with the organization. Other members of the leadership team will "hear the voices of continuous improvement" and accept and support your position on what is being suggested.

Jim Collins, author of *Good to Great,* notes, "Most powerfully transformative executives possess a paradoxical mixture of personal humility and professional will. They are timid and ferocious, shy and fearless, and rare and unstoppable. Good to great transformations do not happen without level five leaders."

According to Stephen R. Covey in his article "Leadership Excellence," organizations are "founded to serve human needs. Successfully working with others makes your knowledge and abilities more productive and facilitates the creation of a complementary team of people who possess knowledge and abilities that can compensate for your weaknesses. Wisdom is the beneficial use of knowledge; wisdom is information and knowledge impregnated with higher purposes and principles. The top people of great organizations are servant leaders. They are the most humble, reverent, open, teachable, respectful, and caring. Leaders must define the organization by reference to core values and purpose; build connection and commitment rooted in freedom of choice, rather than coercion and control; and accept that the exercise of true leadership is inversely proportional to the exercise of power. Organizations are only sustainable when they serve human needs."

You will hear this many, many times during your career, and we know this is not the first time, but great leaders develop a vision. They know where they and the organization are going, and they know how to get there. In addition, everyone who works with this leader has the same knowledge, and everyone is involved. The goose plans for the long flight, is consistent with the formation, does not tire over the duration of the flight, and uses the strengths of his or her associates as they continuously switch places in the formation's lead position.

Every successful organization requires a positive performance in three basic areas: values, direct results, and development of people. The leader's actions validate his or her values. In other words, if you act and behave with leadership values, you have no leadership values. The effective leader is focused on attaining the required results and surrounds herself or himself with good people who, for the most part, were developed from within. These leaders regularly use the plural pronoun "we," rather than the singular pronoun "I."

According to Professor Dave Dow, a worthwhile exercise for emerging leaders is to ask and answer these two questions: "What is being chiseled on my tombstone right now?" and "What is it going to read?" Will you be remembered for serving or being powerful? Rest assured the leaders we remember are those who serve their associates. So, be a leader who makes a difference in people's lives. Remember birthdays and organizational anniversary dates, and continually ask about families and their well-being. Your associates will not forget.

One of our students chose Princess Diana, and gave the class a report as the example for the Historic Leadership Assignment. Princess Diana was truly a servant leader, especially in light of the fact that she was a member of the royal family. The family was known for distancing themselves from their people and traditionally being very reserved. Diana was willing to adapt herself to these ideals and values. She cared about her constituents and put her people first. She was also known for her credibility.

Another student chose Mahatma Gandhi, who was also a servant leader. He was a controversial risk-taker, one who felt so strongly about his beliefs that he was willing to sacrifice everything to obtain justice. He was a true peacemaker and a humble servant of humanity.

ASSESSING YOUR PERSONALITY

What are these personality assessments all about? We are tempted not to share the details of the evaluation processes because they will change in the future or be replaced by more comprehensive assessments. However, further thought leads us to share the details. The Myers-Briggs Personality Assessment is second generation and still widely used. The assessment used by HDS Services had been in place and used for approximately twenty years at the time of the company's acquisition in 2005. The Myers-Briggs Personality Assessment is designed to assist you in understanding your results on the Myers-Briggs Type Indicator (MBTI). The participant is asked to complete the MBTI instrument, and results are produced to identify which of the sixteen different personality types best describe the participant. The personality type represents your preferences in four separate categories, with each category composed of two opposite poles. The categories are:

- **Where you focus your attention**
  Extroversion (E) or Introversion (I)

- **The way you take in information**
  Sensing (S) or Intuition (I)

- **The way you make decisions**
  Thinking (T) or Feeling (F)

- **How you deal with the outer world**
  Judging (J) or Perceiving (P)

We personally participated in the Myers-Briggs Assessment. One of our MBTI types was ESTJ, also described as extroverted, thinking with sensing.

This MBTI result was as follows:

> Reported type: ESTJ
>
> E   is extroversion. Tend to focus attention on the outer world of people and things.
>
> S   is sensing. Tend to take in information through five senses and focus on here and now.

T	is thinking. Tend to make decisions based primarily on logic and objective analysis of cause and effect.
J	is judging. Tend to take a planned approach to life and prefer to have things settled.

Does this mean that these results indicated that the participant is a candidate for leadership excellence? Absolutely not! The results indicate "how" the participant will lead. Someone with the exact opposite results can be an effective leader as well. Are you an effective leader? Some would say: "It depends on who you talk to."

Leaders are perceived differently by diverse associates. Did we get the job done and achieve most of our objectives? Yes, we did! What, then, can prohibit someone from being an effective leader? There are several overriding essentials that are a must to be an effective leader, and those would be integrity/ethics, positive thinking, trust, customer focus, and communication skills.

What kind of leader would the INFP (opposite) participant be?	
I	is introversion. Tend to focus their attention on the inner world of ideas and expressions.
N	is intuition. Tend to take in information from patterns and the big picture, and focus on future possibilities.
F	is feeling. Tend to make decisions based on values and subjective evaluation of person–centered concerns.
P	is perceiving. Tend to like flexibility and spontaneous approach to life, and prefer to keep their options open.
The INFP leader can be effective. This leader would lead in a different way, but could get the same, if not better, results.	

Should the organization's CEO surround herself or himself with a stereotypical "same as the CEO" leadership team? Or, should he/she seek diversity? This CEO would respond with the second alternative. Diversity is an inner strength of an organization that manifests itself in creativity, risk, change, and gain. With diversity there are no barriers and limitless horizons.

The overall description of ESTJ is:

- Decisive, clear, and assertive

- Logical, analytical, and objectively critical

- Adept at organizing projects, procedures, and people

- Values confidence, efficiency, and results

- Prefers proven systems and procedures

- Focused on the present, applying relevant past experience to deal with the issues

- Seen by others as conscientious, dependable, decisive, outspoken, and self-confident. An example of reframing here would be arrogant versus self-confident.

Again, the results of this assessment only identify how you will lead because of your personality that is based on an assessment of your preferences. It does not tell you how effective you will be as a leader. The results of each of the assessments were given to each participant only as private and confidential.

TEAM-BASED PERSONALITY ASSESSMENT

At HDS Services, we occasionally used a personality assessment for all members of our corporate management team and selected members of our management teams in the field. The initial results of the assessment were similar to those of the Myers-Briggs Personality assessment.

There was an added dimension with the assessment used at HDS. Following the identification of the individuals' character and attributes, a reframing exercise took place which outlined how others might perceive you and your attributes. Examples would include a strict person as being inflexible, a neat and organized person as being uptight, or a realistic person as being process and policy oriented.

John H. King, Jr. and Dr. Ronald F. Cichy

KNOWING YOURSELF

At the conclusion of our focus on self, the students provided us with feedback about the course, in general, so that future classes and students could benefit. This was a brainstorming activity. The most common positive comment about the course was how much the students learned about themselves. This was not only the result of the personality assessments, but how, as leaders, they reacted to and resolved the many case studies presented. These were actual experiences compiled over a forty-year career and shared with the students for discussion.

An old Cheyenne Native American proverb states, "Our first teacher is our own heart." In other words, it is important to get to know yourself before attempting to know and learn from others.

Another exercise in knowing one's self is defining and discovering our values. In essence, our life is directed by our values and how we use them when we act. Completing this exercise can help you discover how you want to lead your life, which may be in contrast to your current direction. It is important to live out of the values that are aligned with your purpose. Place a check mark by ten of the following that represent your own values, and then place a second check mark by five of the ten you selected to indicate your top five values. Each value (word) is defined as you define it.

___ Achievement	___ Justice
___ Advancement	___ Knowledge
___ Adventure	___ Leadership
___ Aesthetics	___ Leisure
___ Animals	___ Life
___ Approval	___ Location
___ Autonomy	___ Loyalty
___ Beauty	___ Music
___ Caring	___ Nature
___ Caution	___ Objectivity
___ Challenge	___ Peace
___ Change in Variety	___ Pleasure
___ Children	___ Politics
___ Closeness	___ Power
___ Comfort	___ Precision
___ Companionship	___ Preservation
___ Competition	___ Quality
___ Conformity	___ Quiet
___ Conservation	___ Reading
___ Control	___ Recognition
___ Cooperation	___ Recycling
___ Creativity	___ Relaxation
___ Economic Security	___ Religion
___ Excitement	___ Responsibility
___ Fame	___ Risk
___ Family Happiness	___ Safety
___ Fixing Things	___ Solitude
___ Flexibility	___ Stability
___ Freedom	___ Structure
___ Friendship	___ Talent
___ Fun	___ Teaching
___ Generosity	___ Time/Freedom
___ Growth	___ Timeliness
___ Healthy	___ Trustworthiness
___ Help Others	___ Uniqueness
___ Independence	___ Wealth
___ Inner Harmony	___ Wisdom
___ Integrity	___ Work Ethic
___ Intellectual Status	___ Writing

The top ten values will describe your inner self very well; the top five values give you an even clearer picture as to who you are. Now you have four resources to which to refer. You also have a list of perceptions of how others could see you. These perceptions will surface from time to time in the evaluation process used by your organization's leaders. However, you need to make sure your leaders agree with what you think your inner self is and what your predominant values are. Once aligned, you and your team will excel, and your list of qualities, keys, and secrets will grow.

CHARACTER AND LEADERSHIP

William J. Byron wrote: "There are three adjectives that sum up, in my view, the essential characteristics of leadership. They are accountable, available, and vulnerable." The one leadership quality which is essential is character. Your character is who you are when no one is looking. It is what you do and how you act in secret, when no one else is watching.

It is critical that public and private organizations have a commitment throughout and at the top that reflects organizational ethics and acceptable organizational governance. To repeat, effective leaders take their places at the center of the circle, not the top of the pyramid. From that vantage point, the leaders can best serve their followers by working more closely with them, setting proper examples, and having a better understanding of the issues and challenges facing the associates. Also, humility will get you off to a good start on the path of leadership. If you succeed in the long run to become an effective leader, humility will be there to greet you at the end of a satisfying and productive career.

In an article entitled "Young Sages," Judith Hodgson Carr writes about her interviews with young future leaders and how certain she is that the outlook for the future is bright. During the interview process, the sages made extraordinary observations such as:

- Leaders must set the example.
- To truly lead, one must set the tone by actions, not words.
- The organization must not just be a place to work, but each member of the team should be part of the whole, of the greater good.
- Believe in others, never let teammates settle for anything less than the best.
- Empathy is a characteristic of a leader.
- Organizations promote the good of the community and self as well.

- Faith, hope, love, and fierce determination are characteristics of a leader.

Strong leaders have a personal vision and set of values, and align with the same for the organization they lead. These are what the leader stands for and what drives the leader and the organization.

The key lessons learned in this chapter are that any person with any of the assessed personality traits can be developed to become an effective leader. In fact, the organization's CEO should surround himself or herself with varying personalities, thus forming a diverse team of executives. Diversity creates strength through innovation, change, creativity, risk taking, thinking out of the box, being first to market, and being the organization of choice.

CHAPTER THREE

REFERENCES

Anonymous. Cheyenne Native American proverb.

Byron, William J. "The Tools and Qualities of Effective Leadership." *Vital Speeches of the Day*, August 2003, 60 (20): 639.

Carr, Judith H. "Young Sages." *Association Management*, August 1995, 47 (8): 107–11.

Cichy, Ronald F. "Leadership: Understand Yourself First." *The Journal of the National Association of College & University Food Service*, 1999, 21:100–06.

Collins, Jim. *Good to Great*. New York: HarperCollins, 2001.

Covey, Stephen. "Servant Leadership." *Leadership Excellence*, December 2006, 23 (12): 5–6.

HDS Services. A Management Profile Assessment (CD-ROM), July 2007. Prof. King, Would you give me more detail information on this?

Myers, Isabel B., and Peter B. Myers. *Gifts Differing: Understanding Personality Type*. Mountain View, CA: Davis-Black Publishing, 1980, 1995.

Chapter Four
Integrity and Honesty

Leadership and Integrity

When asked to prepare a list of great leaders as perceived by others, not all would necessarily be good, ethical people. Some recent executives, including CEOs who pretended to be leaders, would be on the list, but they may also not be good. They would be added to the list that includes Bin Laden, Attila, Stalin, Hitler, and Saddam Hussein. Each of these leaders failed the ultimate test of being honest. Their communication was littered with one falsehood after another. Dr. Spencer Johnson, author of *Who Moved My Cheese*, said, "Integrity is telling myself the truth, and honesty is telling the truth to other people." We agree.

Some of the individuals on the list are good people gone bad. When it was time to take a stand and do the right thing, they failed. Great leaders not only possess admirable values; they have the courage to take the stand by acting on the values others admire and take the organization or team down the path of integrity and honesty. These are also leaders who always consider the long-range results or consequences of their decisions and actions. Unfortunately, it only takes a few bad apples to ruin the perception people have of leaders, in general. Some leaders in the political arena do not assist in changing this negative paradigm. Oftentimes when politicians and the media get together, there is not much positive to report. So, we would strongly suggest that you separate your opinions of political leadership and organizational leadership.

A mentor once advised to always perform in such a way that the true test of integrity is what you would do if no one would ever know. Leaders have to answer to their own personal set of values. Some would say this may be easier said than done. But without a set of values, you have no foundation on which to base your decisions, allocate your time, or use your resources. You will make decisions based on circumstances, pressures, or your moods at the time. In Barack Obama's book *Dreams from My Father*, he described his humble start in life, and the morals that were placed with him when he was little and were still with him as he got older. His mother told him at a young age that he needed to have values. She detailed them as honesty, fairness, straight talk, and independent judgment.

Leaders live in a totally different environment and must live by the highest of ethical standards. After all, they only get one chance. One misuse of the position and the resulting loss of trust means that they must suffer the consequences, losing their leadership positions, and probably never being actively involved as a leader again. In some cases there could be prison time and loss of family. How would you start over with a terribly blemished record? The environment where leaders lead is similar to a fish bowl. They can be seen 24 hours a day, seven days a week, and 365 days a year; they are always held to a higher level of ethical behavior. When they fail to make the right ethical decisions, they fail as a leader and everyone will know about it. However, the flip side is that a high level of respect and trust is gained when the leader takes a stand and selects the most ethical option, even though it might be unpopular. As a leader, you should always do what is best for the organization and team as a whole, and base your decisions on what the customer would do if they were making the decision.

One of the exercises we use in our Emerging Leadership class involves the students selecting a book that details the life of a great leader, reviewing the information, and making a presentation to the entire class. Each time we teach the class, we use this Historic Leader Assignment and presentation. The title of the book chosen by one of the students was *Ronald Reagan: How an Ordinary Man Became an Extraordinary Leader*. In addition to being a visionary, Reagan was incorruptible and cared nothing about personal glory. He had a sign on his desk at the White House that read: "There is no limit to what a person can do or where he can go if he does not mind who gets the credit." This student said, "When I learn about something that I value, and hear it from the mouth of a leader like Ronald Reagan that I respect, it solidifies in my mind that what I value is of the utmost importance. It reassures me that I am on the right track and to continue on. An overall sense of confidence can be felt, which in turn will increase the chances of being successful along my journey as an emerging leader. One of the greatest things I have learned from Reagan is to follow your heart."

DEALING WITH PRESSURE

The most common root cause of "good people gone bad" is pressure. In today's business environment there is blistering pressure to meet the financial expectations of leadership and stakeholders. This has been allowed to filter down to senior leaders and managers, and this is where the heart of the problem initiates. Some leaders find ways to increase the bottom line, resulting in happy shareholders, higher shares value, and more lucrative bonus payouts. The most amazing point in all of the recent cases of good people gone bad is that all of their organizations possessed a code of ethics and extensive external controls.

Now, after all of the fallout, the focus at these and other organizations has shifted to what is happening inside the organization. Organizations are now searching for internal problems that act as barriers to doing things ethically, as barriers to promoting communication of misconduct associates observe, and as a possible incentive to make an unethical decision. Reporting unethical behavior must be part of the organization's culture.

Noel Tichy and Warren Bennis, who authored the article "Wise Leaders" state: "Pressure can pull us away from our core values, just as they are reinforced by our success in the market. Some people refer to this as 'CEO-itis.' Ironically, the more successful some executives are, the more tempted they are to take short cuts. Then, the rewards, compensation, stock option gains, executive perks, positive media stories, and admiring comments from peers all reinforce our actions and drive to keep it going."

ORGANIZATIONAL CULTURE

So what is culture? It is a snapshot of the in-depth evaluation of the organization, good or bad. When the values and behaviors of all the associates—bottom to top—are totaled, you have the culture of the organization.

Organizations and their leaders must protect themselves by having a strong ethics governance group consisting of leadership and strong, detached legal counsel to protect against behaviors such as conflict of interest, harassment, gifting, and other unethical practices. The organization's annual audit must be thorough and conducted independently and objectively, at arm's length without bias.

Establishing a Code of Ethics

What is a code of ethics? At HDS Services we called it the "Code of Management and Business Practices." It outlined the assigned individuals on the team that monitor compliance and deal with ethical issues. Usually, the organization's general counsel heads up the team, with other members usually being members of the board's executive committee, including the human resources officer.

The policies of the code addressed compliance with law, organization records, conflict of interest, independent business decisions (no confusion), proprietary information, political activities, ethical procedures, equal opportunity, harassment, gifts, and client relations. Also included in the code were reporting instructions, enforcement, and code distribution recommendations. The code served as the guide for all associates from top to bottom on how to behave and make ethical decisions. The organization's expectations on ethics were outlined in detail.

The HDS Corporate Business Practices Team minimally met on an annual basis. The agenda consistently included a review of the current code, its effectiveness, and its applicability to the company/industry operations. Each and every management associate in the organization was completely oriented to the code's existence and detailed content. However, and equally important, was the orientation to the HDS culture which promoted the freedom to express one's views and opinions, and particularly in this case, encouragement to be the "whistle-blower" in the event of a code violation, regardless of who the offender was.

Seven Keys to Organizational Ethical Success

According to David Gebler in his article "Creating an Ethical Culture," there are seven keys to organizational ethical success.

1. **First and foremost is the financial stability of the organization.** This is where many executives get into trouble attempting to impress shareholders and their board of directors. They become overly creative with accounting practices and cross the line of ethical behavior. This is especially true when it involves associate bonuses based in financial incentives. It could be as simple as booking income or overhead cost in the month or year which will qualify the individual for a more lucrative bonus. Organizations that are ethical and profitable have an ethical chief financial officer and team,

and do not fall into the trap of making exceptions to strong accounting principles and procedures.

> I have personally been in executive meetings where requests were made to bend the rules to accommodate both internal and external customers. These decisions are what lead to unethical practices, a lack of trust and respect for the leadership of the organization, and eventually serious problems for the organization as a whole, including going out of business.

2. **Excellent communication throughout the organization** is also essential, because this limits what certain individuals may otherwise get away with, including unethical behaviors. This supports the whistle-blower option for all associates. This communication tool or policy serves the interests of all associates, leaders, and the organization as a whole, and also includes suppliers and customers. The seriousness of the infraction must be weighed very carefully before stepping forward with the information. The key to the success of the whistle-blower option rests with the culture of the organization, because the associates have to trust the leadership of the organization to be ethical in dealing with issues. If leadership fails to support the whistle-blower, the other associates will not stay with the organization very long. This is where the value of intelligence capital becomes a central focus. Your associates will be the organization's most important asset, because without them the organization has nothing.

3. **Strong internal controls** must also be in place. These processes are added and refined over the years through the continuous improvement process. Most controls are procedural in nature and must be known and practiced by all associates. Control systems are established which automatically warn leadership that nonconforming activity is taking place. When the activity becomes known, it is vital that immediate action take place. The leader must make certain that everyone realizes he or she is extremely serious.

4. **Accountability** also plays a key role because everyone must be responsible for their individual actions. Full knowledge of the content of the code and a sense of strong responsibility for their actions drive accountability by everyone in the organization. This is where many leaders make the serious mistake of thinking of themselves as to never being questioned by associates and customers. They believe they are above all, and do not have to worry about having their integrity questioned. The reality is that leaders are more apt to be scrutinized, and, in fact, live in a fishbowl. In

addition, leaders are targets for inappropriate behavior for many reasons, including the perception that they have deep pockets and can be sued.

5. Organizations where **vision is revisited annually and is aligned** with an associate's personal vision seldom cross over the ethics line. Reviewing the vision entails visiting the organization's core values, which should mirror each associate's personal values. The associate's annual performance evaluation must include a comparative review of his or her personal core values.

    Many associates experience changes in their core values from year to year because they are positively or negatively influenced by external sources and occurrences. The review will lead to discussions regarding the organization's position on ethical issues.

6. Also, **organizations which are tightly connected with their respective communities** seldom get into trouble because most of the inner workings of the organization are well known throughout the community. Community leadership includes many highly ethical individuals and groups that informally form an effective team of watchdogs.

7. And lastly, organizations must **consider the long-term impact of an ethics problem**. Organizations must be sustainable. Rumors and small insignificant incidents can damage an organization's reputation, which results in decreasing sales and possible financial problems.

Recovery from organizational ethics scandals is difficult at best. The Tyco investigation in 2002 led to conviction on 22 of 23 counts faced by the CEO. What are most important in this example are what actions new leadership took to turn the company around. The new CEO got rid of 290 of the 300 person management team, and set the highest standards of organizational governance, which included accountability, compliance, and integrity. In 2002, Tyco's rating by GMI (Governance Metrics International) was 1.5 on a scale of 10, and, following their governance efforts, this changed to 9.0 in 2005.

Another contributing factor to the organizational ethics outbreak at the turn of the century was the management style portrayed and practiced by many CEOs. The best CEOs in the past were heavily involved with their associates. Hands-on leaders have always been the most successful, but for many reasons there became fewer of them as the end of the twentieth century approached. CEOs became untouchable and unapproachable. Associates became convinced that their bosses were crooks and were totally disillusioned, according to Peter Drucker, the management sage. This is the reason organizations must include "best-in-class reputation" as one of their key organizational objectives.

> HDS Services worked diligently for many years to earn its best-in-class reputation among the food service contract companies. The value of this reputation was enormous when negotiating the divestiture to the Compass Group.

CHALLENGES LEADERS FACE

Every individual seeking a leadership position must realize that personal values and ethical standards will be challenged throughout the leader's career. The leader must have friends and mentors they can count on for advice when the challenge presents itself. It is very likely that an ethical challenge will occur with all leaders. Oftentimes, the advice is garnered from a CFO or the organization's general counsel. But, the underlying values that set your ethics compass must be in place and strong 100 percent of the time. Again, keep in mind that **all** leaders face challenges of this nature during their careers. It will occur in your tenure as a manager and leader. So, be prepared to deal with it well in advance.

PROCESSES SUPPORT ETHICS

We have already established that a strong ethics program will not guarantee ethical behavior in the organization. It has to be supported by ethics-based processes. Also, the organization must evaluate and understand where it may be vulnerable to risk. One way to determine this is to engage consultants, public accountants, auditors, and legal staff to conduct an evaluation. Remember, the more associates know about what is going on, the greater the chance that ethical behavior will prevail. Also of importance is the premise that the process must start at the board of director's level, and both leadership and management must support those who report unethical behavior.

EXAMPLES OF ETHICS VIOLATIONS

It would be useful to review some examples of the more common and less significant violations involving associates on ethical behavior. In Curtis Verschoor's article in *Strategic Finance* entitled "Strong Ethics is a Critical Quality of Leadership," he lists results of a survey published in the *Ethics*

Monitor of Fast Company. "Activities include inflating forecast numbers (12%), taking office supplies home (69%), inflating organization sales to win a client (13%), putting a personal cost on an expense report or corporate credit card (19%), or booking an order that was not yet contracted (6%). The rationalization for these acts included: I do so much for the organization so they owe me these little things; I needed a loan; I did it to buy time to keep my job; and There was pressure from executives to perform."

HOW TO ACT IN UNETHICAL SITUATIONS

How do you as an associate, supervisor, manager, or member of the leadership team handle the situation when confronted with unethical behavior? Basically it is quite simple. First, take a stand on the matter and voice your objection, then propose an alternative action. If not resolved, take the matter up the organizational ladder.

What can you use to serve as a guide for making the right decision when confronted by the temptation to do something that is not ethical? Obviously, your values are your primary guide, but there are other resources as well.

You can use laws as a guide. If you are ignorant of the law, that is no justification for unethical behavior. But, as a good manager you should make sure you know all of the laws pertaining to your position. Also, get to know the foundations or intentions behind the laws. One of the basic principles of leadership is that when you have no faith in the messenger, you will never believe them. And, you will not believe the messenger if you do not know what the messenger's values are. Associates want and expect leaders to articulate their values. These values influence the decisions we make every day and strengthen our commitment to goals and moral judgment. In a nutshell, those values are our personal bottom line. You will have many opportunities throughout your tenure as a leader to let every associate in the organization know exactly what your values are, both by your words as well as by your actions.

Let your conscience be your guide. Listen to the voice within. All managers and leaders know or knew someone in their life that they considered a strong role model. Sometimes, it is helpful to visualize this and ask, "What would he/she have done in this particular situation?" Remember, it is the leader's behavior that wins the respect of associates. There is nothing wrong with being a model and opening the heart to what you believe and think. Also remember that your consistent actions and deeds speak volumes more than your words. Spend time with your associates working at their side and making your values come alive. Associates will always first follow the leader before following a policy or plan.

Rules and procedures should be your guide as well. Procedures are key directions for determining what is right. Abiding by them will assure success, stability, and ethical behavior.

Perhaps most importantly, your personal value system is a guide as well. Our values are well intended and are meant to be used in situations where we can avoid getting into a lot of trouble.

LEADERSHIP LESSON FROM THE EAGLE

Here is a "Leadership Lesson from the Eagle" that is apropos at this time: "To be predictably known as the best is every leader's vision. But, your organization should never become predictable from a strategic point of view. Change will be driven by your actions, but never sacrifice your values for change."

As a new graduate or a young manager, you will possess some of the qualities, keys, and secrets of leadership. You may not necessarily possess all of the characteristics necessary to be a strong leader, but you will more than likely exhibit them to some degree or have the potential to be there based on having practiced some of the basic characteristics. These characteristics demonstrate how you will lead, and include integrity, confidence, passion, commitment, trust, sincerity, customer focus, positive attitude, and courage.

The tools that you use to lead reinforce how you lead. Examples include communication, relationship building, strategic thinking, change making, mentoring, and technology.

Chapter Four

References

Gebler, David. "Creating an Ethical Culture." *Strategic Finance*, May 2006, 87 (11): 29–34.

Johnson, Spencer. *Who Moved My Cheese*. New York: Putnam and Sons Publishing, 1998.

Schlender, Brent. "Interview of Peter Drucker." *Fortune*, January 2004, 149 (1): 114–18.

Tichy, Noel. and Warren Bennis. "Wise Leaders." *Leadership Excellence*, January 2008, 25 (1): 3–4.

Verschoor, Curtis. "Strong Ethics is a Critical Quality of Leadership." *Strategic Finance*, January 2006, 87 (7): 19–20.

Chapter Five
Know Others

Knowing and Serving Others

Now that you understand the importance of knowing *you* and your emotions and feelings, we need to learn who *others* are and how to serve them. This is what servant leaders do. They are humble and very caring leaders. They take communication to a higher level and practice good listening skills. Also, we need to know who *others* are, because as a leader we are called to serve and get input from many different types of customers. As a manager we deal with every customer of the organization with the exception of the stakeholders.

Other Groups Leaders Engage

As a leader, we have additional *others*. One additional group is the owners/ investors (shareholders). The majority of these owners/investors is seldom known by the organization's associates and leaders, unless they are active in the organization or own a significant number of shares. Regardless, they are customers and must be treated as such.

Another group we must pay attention to, and be active in, is the community. This involves volunteering to help the community with its goals and initiatives. A growing community can provide the organization with resources that support the organization's associates, recruitment efforts, and the organization's marketing efforts.

Morrison Management Specialists (MMS), the organization that acquired HDS Services, has an excellent record of community support. MMS associates in Atlanta, Ga., where the corporate offices are located, build a house every two years for a needy family. Also, because of their major presence in the Louisiana market, they played a noticeable role in supporting victims of Hurricane Katrina in 2006.

The other customers include the leader's family, where creation of a balanced life is critical. In the *Managing for Quality* book, we emphasized our leadership commitment to "family first." Although seldom a real occurrence, effective leaders recognize the importance of family over work. Many CEOs are proponents of family/work balance and bring many new ideas and cultural changes to their organization. You will have many opportunities as a leader to make decisions that favor the family over the organization. We will further discuss balance and quality life later in this chapter. The common threads with all of these customer groups are the service (servant leader) approach and the hands-on approach required of leadership. How they serve each group is dramatically different. However, keep in mind the importance of being results oriented and the ability to hold everyone accountable.

SERVING THE ASSOCIATE GROUP

Let us start with the associate group. If a leader is to be successful, he or she must accept the fact that the associates are responsible for the leader's and organization's success, not the other way around. This is why good leaders adopt an associates-first mantra. The Ritz-Carlton philosophy says it all: "Involve associates in the planning of the work that affects them, and they will take pride and joy in their work." The mere fact that we relate to associates as customers means we are serving them. We serve them by listening to them for their ideas, criticism, and suggestions for improvement. They are the creators and deliverers of service to external customers and are the individuals who can best identify the needs and expectations of our customers. Knowing these customers' needs makes it rather simple for the associates to identify the gaps in meeting expectations.

In addition to communication, empowering our associates through mentoring, providing the resources, then getting out of the way, sends a strong servant leader-oriented message. And lastly, display a strong, caring attitude toward them by being interested in their welfare. Effective leaders are in touch with those who are around them. Some leaders refer to this as being compassionate or being a servant leader. If you are going to be compassionate, you have to demonstrate a sense of genuine interest in and curiosity about associates and their experiences. You have to want to learn as much as you can about your associates and be willing to take the appropriate action when necessary. Be careful not to confuse caring with sympathy. And remember that one of the pillars of effective leadership is communication, which largely is based on good listening skills. In addition, you will be challenged to create a compassionate culture in your organization through the vision and setting the example. Be hands-on, use management by walking around (MBWA), and recognize all achievements regardless of the extent of impact.

All leaders must be willing to help the associate achieve their goals. The more someone is emotionally involved with the associate's life, the more susceptible they will be to being influenced by the mentor. On the other hand, the associate should be open to suggestions and the mentoring process in general. The associate should select the most successful people in the areas where they require the most help. Associates will have many mentors at any given time, but they need to remember that mentors are willing to work with them only if the associates are making progress. The bottom line is that the more you help others, the more they will assist you. A very simple way to achieve a high level of learning in your organization is to follow this advice: "Tell me, and I will forget. Show me, and I may remember. Involve me, and I will understand."

This takes us back to learning, being mentored, mentoring, and respect for the effective leader. Ask yourself who you have the most respect for among all those people you have worked with over the years. Ninety percent of these people are those who taught you the most about managing, leading, and the industry in which you work. So, it makes sense to turn this around and be an excellent mentor to gain respect from your associates.

SERVING EXTERNAL CUSTOMERS

Serving an external customer is somewhat different, but not in the case of expectations. Both external customers and associates (i.e., internal customers) have unique expectations, but learning what their needs are is basically the same. For the customer (in our business, we call them clients), we are attempting to develop a long-term partnership where the two organizations assist each other in achieving their objectives.

> There were many examples of this with HDS, but one stands out because of the positive impact on each organization. This was a long-standing client when we were first approached to assist with catering a seasonal event, "The Festival of Trees," using the floor of a hockey arena. Attendance was anticipated at over one thousand. It was a high-end cocktail party serving seafood, tenderloin, and other upscale hors d'oeuvres at multiple stations. All of the prepreparation had to be done off-site at the client facility. HDS Services brought in thirty to forty chefs, servers, assistant managers, supervisors, and others to work the party. We only charged the client for the food, supplies, and rental expense. There was no charge for the personnel. This event would have cost the client $60,000 to $80,000 if served by another reputable high-end caterer. Over the years, the event grew, and our commitment did as well. In the true spirit of a partnership, and, realizing this client account would be an excellent training facility, we requested that the client permit HDS the ability and approval to train and develop assistant managers at the facility without concern for length of assignment. We received their approval, and this was certainly a positive change for HDS.

Effective customer communication and knowledge of customer expectations are essential ingredients in the serving leadership scenario. Continuous improvement is also key. *Effective communication, knowing and exceeding expectations, and continuous improvement are the foundation for serving* others. The partnership that develops is the extension of service that creates loyalty in both parties.

SERVING OWNERS AND INVESTORS

Often the leader's bosses are the owners and investors in the organization and represent an *other* customer group. Effective communication with mentors is essential but in a substantially different and less frequent way. It consists of monthly or quarterly reporting and detailed annual reports that include highlights of the strategic plan, some forecasts for the upcoming year, and an analysis of the organization's market share. Never forget that the leader will have to stand before the shareholders each year and answer questions about his or her performance, personal goals, where the organization has been, and where the organization is going. This annual meeting is no place for unexpected major announcements or surprises for the shareholders.

SERVING SUPPLIERS

Suppliers as *other* customers make great partners and can bring a strong strategic advantage to the organization. Rather than "beating up suppliers," the goal is to work with suppliers as strategic partners to improve their products and services, so they can improve their position in their industry and assist our organization with improved products and services. Most organizations have suppliers who are considered "prime suppliers," which indicates that this supplier provides anywhere from 80 to 100 percent of purchased products in a given segment of the overall purchasing portfolio. These are the suppliers we must develop to allow them to reach a partnership level. In the food services industry, such as that of HDS Services, the suppliers are asked to improve such things as fill rates, product returns, distribution arrival compliancy, pricing, and special services such as providing mobile storage of products for major client events or providing products that are not normally distributed by the supplier, such as a onetime purchase of an Asian product from Beijing, China. Working with prime suppliers by consolidating the volume of products to preferred manufacturers is a strong partnership strategy that has a tremendous positive financial impact on product pricing.

> At HDS Services we annually recognized the efforts of our supplier partners at a first-class golf outing sponsored by our organization. We would invite about seventy people who represented the vendor group. They were from all regions of the country, and most participated because this was an unusual practice on the part of a customer. It was a one-day event at a prestigious private club in the Detroit area. The skill of participants ranged from golf professional to beginner. Not only was it a fun event, it was a demonstration of the partnership as a reality. Many of the vendor participants were competitors of one another and were not hesitant to recognize the partnership with HDS Services and their appreciation for our unique relationship.

SERVING THE COMMUNITY

In addition to the associates, customers, shareholders, family, and suppliers, leaders are acutely aware of their responsibilities for community efforts. We have previously mentioned efforts to support hurricane victims and those community members unable to provide their families with housing. Relationships with the various communities where our organization is located and conducts business are critical to long-term-success. The image and perception of the organization will go a long way to solidify sustainability and organizational growth.

> This brings to mind an e-mail Morrison Management Specialists leadership team members received from Scott MacClellan, the CEO. He wrote: "This week we had a potential coffee supplier present to us. This company was founded by Harvard Business School grads with the idea they could create a company that was driven and focused but also create 'compassion capitalism'—economic systems that help change lives. This company, for example, put farmers to work for coffee beans rather than drugs and built schools and soccer fields for the children of the coffee bean farmers. While it is a for-profit company, it is owned by a not-for-profit that takes the profits and donates them to charitable causes. Knowing each of you, I thought you would resonate with this idea. Knowing you, I know that is what you would like to do with Morrison. I believe that we can change the world for the better by supporting organizations that practice socially responsible business activities, leaving economic systems that support life for our children, and earth-friendly practices that leave a planet better than we found it. I believe we can build a better world by caring for the health and wellness of our associates, customers, and guests. Morrison can practice compassion capitalism."

Remember that most of our customers are the "end users" of our products and services. These consumers have a much different view of the word "profit" than the people on Wall Street or the executives in the boardroom. These individual consumers have a perception of profit that it is necessary but also believe that the employer should do something to share some of the profits with its associates. So, when an organization is actively involved with the community in giving back, the perceptions change for the most part. The community members now see the organization as one that cares about them, their families, and the community, in general. So, how should leaders manage the word *profit?* Basically the key is how you go about making the profit or how you conduct business to reach your financial goals. The best way to manage this is to give your associates a voice in the vision, mission, and the values—the way the organization is managed and led. When you empower your associates and get out of their way, the profits will become a reality without leadership having to continually push for improved numbers.

SERVING YOUR FAMILY

The family *other* is by far the most important, but we need to discuss *self* first. You need to answer some key questions such as:

- What do I want to create in my life?

- If my life were ideal, what would be happening, and how would I know it?

- What are my dreams for my life in the future?

- What are my dreams for my family, and how do I best balance work and family expectations?

The best way to manage the expectations of family is to base all family decisions on consideration of three factors: self, significant others, and work. All decisions should be balanced using all three of these factors.

If all members of the family are committed to the relationship, balancing work and family will be successful. Like the management principles outlined in chapter two, these also pertain to family. The principles include having a vision (family dream), removing inspection, continuous improvement, no fear, no barriers, process thinking, team approach, and vigorous support for education, celebrating and recognizing success, and maintaining balance. Family members must treat others with dignity, avoid behaviors and feelings that impair the relationships, contribute to the family dream, share basic values based on trust and respect, teach and mentor others, assess self and significant others, promote cooperation, and have a positive outlook.

Our other leader, the Eagle, shares these words in a leadership lesson: "Do things as a family whenever possible so the children can view first-hand how to correctly resort to real-life situations, issues, and challenges. As a leader, you will be living in a fishbowl, so take advantage by setting good examples."

Colin Powell, as reported by Oren Harari, believes that "perpetual optimism is a force multiplier, but so are cynicism and pessimism." We need to push change and eliminate negative thinking that fears change. What happens if the leader pushes "we can be the best" and we do not reach our goals? This is easily resolved in the beginning by making certain that everyone understands this is a journey and to be the best may take forever. What is important is continuing to improve in small incremental steps that move the organization closer to being "the best."

Remember that people do not resist change. They resist being told to change.

CHAPTER FIVE

REFERENCES

Harari, Oren. *The Leadership Secrets of Colin Powell.* New York: McGraw Hill, 2002.

Part III

Building Leadership Skills

Chapter Six–
The Effective Manager

"Remember that you are too blessed to be stressed."

Chapter Seven–
Leading with Emotional
Intelligence

"You don't have to win every argument. Agree to disagree."

Chapter Eight–
Planning and Building Your
Career

"You cannot get swept off your feet if you are sitting down. Stand up and be noticed."
Claire Camden

"Do not compare your life to others. You have no idea what their journey is all about."

Chapter Six
The Effective Manager

Questions of the Unknown

Imagine that today you have arrived at your first management position. There are hundreds of questions running through your mind. Have I made the right choice of organizations? What will my first boss really be like? Will he or she be a smothering, distrustful follow-up artist, or a great mentor who is effective at delegation? Will age be a barrier to achieving my aspirations?

What about the team of associates who will be working with me and will be twice my age? Will they think I am just another book-smart college graduate? Will they hold it against me because I was promoted from within, and they were not? Will they disrespect me because I am unfamiliar with many of the tasks they perform? Or if we used to work together as associates, how will they treat me as the new manager of that same team? How should I act or respond if the associates respond to me negatively?

How to Handle the Unknown

In the two to three years as a student, intern, or associate many have learned much of the basics of being a successful manager, and they trust that they will be managed by their new organization's team with these same essentials. Many remember nearly everything that they have learned about what their management demeanor should be in supervising their first team of associates. In a nutshell, treat them with respect and humility. Let them know that you can learn the many intricacies of the industry from them. Genuinely care about them and their families. Decisions will be team-based rather than solely the manager's to make. Every decision will be based on what is best for the associates *and* for the organization as a whole. Genuine leaders do not make up a response to associate questions, because it will damage the trust and integrity. Challenges certainly exist in managing those associates who are close to your age, the generation Y group. The basics are the same; however, the associates are different and need choices; plus, they are totally tuned in to technology. As Robin Lee Allen wrote in the article "Managers Must Set Example for Gen Y Kidployees": "Employers must get inside their heads and think like them."

Effective managers manage by walking around (MBWA) and give recognition frequently and personally. They do not wait for the annual awards ceremony. They encourage creativity and suggestions for change, and, as Oren Harari quotes Colin Powell: "We must discourage 'yes men' because, if you have a yes man, one of you is redundant." Of course, this also applies to "yes women."

Effective Management

Before you begin the management phase of the leadership journey, you must have a clear understanding of the differences between yesterday's management culture and managing an effective team, department, or organization in today's environment. All studies and research have made it clear that today's "best" manager is more successful by being customer focused, working to prevent problems and hassles, having a goal of 100 percent customer satisfaction, knowing that a commitment to excellence is critical in each process, using team synergies, welcoming criticism and all ideas for change, promoting empowerment throughout their span of control, keeping the ego in check because they do not know it all (time to learn), and not being afraid of hard work. As Yogi Berra once said, "You give 100 percent in the first half of the game, and if that is not enough, in the second half, you give the rest."

This table outlines the differences between yesterday's traditional manager and the effective manager you want to emulate.

Table One: The Effective Manager Matrix

INDICATOR	TRADITIONAL MANAGER	THE EFFECTIVE MANAGER
Foundation of Goals	Expectations of Organization's Leader	Needs of All Customers
Issue Resolution	Issues are Detected After the Fact	Problems are Prevented by Proactive Management
Customer Satisfaction	Leader's Goals for Margins of Error and Waste are Published	Accept Nothing Less than 100% Satisfaction
Achieving Quality Services and Products	Inspect Quality In	Commit to Quality in All Processes
Organizational Response to Problems	Independent competing Silos (teams)	Use Cooperative Cross-functional Teams
Management-Associate Relationship	Top-down Direction	Associate Participation and Empowerment at All Levels
Organization's No.1 Goal	Short-term Profits	Long-term Organizational Success

There are many differences between the actions of yesterday's managers and today's managers, who face many new challenges. It begins with the common organizational goals related to bottom-line profits which were the sole driving force years ago. Today, managers must focus their attention on the success of their associates and organizational sustainability, both originating with customers.

So you can clearly see that successful organizations are driven by customers' needs rather than the directives of the organization's leadership. The need for continuous change remains a priority, but we now utilize self–directed teams to facilitate improvements. Yesterday's management would departmentalize change, which is now referred to as functioning within silos, meaning only your department's best interests. In addition, and in response to escalating customer expectations, managers must seek continuous improvement when it comes to eliminating problems. This is obviously a major paradigm shift from the twentieth century principles of management.

Having reviewed the habits and principles of the effective manager, please acknowledge that this is what you want to be as you develop and master your management skills. Even if every member of your supervisory team possesses the characteristics of the effective manager, you will have a diverse team because all individuals have a unique set of paradigms, skills, competencies, and abilities. The more diverse your team is, the more productive and creative they will be in serving your customers. You will need to meet with your supervisors right away to identify both sets (yours and theirs) of expectations. And, it should not take long to learn their capabilities so you can align these with the appropriate responsibilities and perhaps change these responsibilities based on individual skills. Today's most effective managers place associates in roles that are aligned with their individual strengths. In other words, put them in a position where they can succeed.

As a manager you will be faced with challenges you have not encountered before. You will need to have the courage to make the appropriate decisions, which could include laying individuals off or moving people who are antagonistic obstructionists and do not work well in teams. The wise leader knows every associate very well and is committed to keeping the teams together and productive. Most associates will support team decisions, but when they do not, the manager must have the courage to take action in the name of continuous improvement. And lastly, consult your team when making the tough decisions and never take the position of "if it is not broken, do not fix it."

LEARNING FROM SUCCESSFUL LEADERS

In our leadership class, students are asked to complete an historic leader assignment, including selecting an autobiography or biography of a leader whom they admire, and report about that chosen leader. One student chose Lance Armstrong's book, *It's Not About the Bike: My Journey Back to Life*. Lance presents details about never giving up when race conditions are tough or when fighting cancer. Everyone must stick to the cause. Another student chose Markel's account of Rudy Giuliani's book, *Leadership*. She was impressed with his encouraging others to be accountable and his preparing the team every day for the challenges ahead.

Fortunately, there is a better way: rather than quitting, you could undergo a management strategy paradigm shift. A paradigm is an outstandingly clear or typical example—an archetype. It is an original model or pattern of which all things of the same type are representations. In other words, management paradigms are the eyeglasses through which managers view the world. The difficult situation some managers find themselves in illustrates a typical management paradigm. An alternative paradigm requires you to view management as innovation. In the alternative model, the one we call effective management, you will see change occurring and want to help make it happen. Early assignments may seem to be mundane or trivial, so be sure to give your best effort. At the very least, the manager accepts change early.

A Real World Paradigm Shift

In 1991, several senior operations executives approached the president of HDS Services, a food services management company, and informed him that HDS was falling behind in the area of quality services and products. Corporate standards were excellent, but the systems, techniques, and processes required to achieve these standards were noticeably missing. The organization had been experiencing some difficulty competing in certain high-profile retail markets, and the new managers on board did not possess the same standards of excellence that senior management had developed over the years.

This senior operations team convinced the president that there could be value in attending a presentation in Chicago on the principles of quality improvement. They attended the conference, returned to the corporate office, and convinced the team that the organization should seriously consider adopting this quality effort. This experience was virtually responsible for a massive paradigm shift within HDS Services, which was to a focus on managing for quality. A quality improvement presentation was made to the executives of HDS Services in October 1991, and the content of this presentation was well received by the team and made a lasting impression on everyone. Many quality-related management tools and principles had never been used at HDS Services. The basic principles of quality management had never been formally practiced. There was not even a formal vision or company mission statement.

We decided to accept the challenge of transforming HDS into a quality-improvement company and took a formal adoption recommendation to the Executive Staff Committee, which was a nine-member committee responsible for developing corporate policy, long-range planning, and finalizing the annual strategic plan. We and a group of associates developed the plan in

---

merely two weeks and presented it to the committee. The question was whether we could adopt totally new management principles, and put them into action in a company with many operational paradigms. Could we shift to a bottom-up management style throughout the organization? As it turned out, the committee was more than ready for change. It was a unanimous vote to move forward. A skeletal implementation plan was developed that very day, and soon a financial impact analysis was developed. The return on investment could be achieved by the end of 1992. Returns would be generated in the form of associate productivity, increased sales, and general savings in overhead.

Before the end of 1991, the president took the plan to the Executive Committee of the board. The entire plan was discussed in detail by this three-person group, and the focus was whether the board could change their management paradigm. The plan was approved immediately. As it turned out, HDS was a team of change makers, not change fighters.

STEPS TO MAKING CHANGE

When making changes in the way you or your organization conduct business, you should take the time to do it right. There are three stages in the change process: ending the old, a time of neutrality to experiment and learn, and a new start with no barriers and total support. There are no recommended time guidelines, as some changes will naturally require more time. The manager will know when it is the right time if there are open communications within the team.

Step One: Ending the Old

In ending the old process, with which you are very comfortable, you must be very clear about what is ending. Be honest with yourself and evaluate what you may lose due to the shift. Do not assume what is and what might be; be totally objective in your assessment. As the next step, place closure on the old process.

Step Two: A Time of Neutrality

In the neutral or learning phase, you may feel frustrated or misplaced, thinking you are not even working for the same organization any more. This is perfectly normal, and it will eventually come to an end. Do not become paralyzed by this loss of direction. The keys to a successful shift are great communication, recognizing the progress of your associates, and a willingness to be creative.

Step Three: Take the Time to Do It Right

Do not begin to implement the change until you and your associates are ready and fully prepared. Your team should have a mission statement prepared outlining how you plan to achieve your transformation. Everyone must act as if there were no barriers and be open to request and accept assistance along the way. So, why is change so important, and what does it have to do with managing for quality? First, we need to define what quality is and clarify for all the models we want to pursue.

DEFINING THE MANAGING FOR QUALITY MODEL

What is the Managing for Quality model? Twenty years ago, the response would be Total Quality Management (TQM). The immediate perception would have been a scientific, numbers-related management model. This is definitely not what we are talking about in our Managing for Quality model. We are talking about using and practicing management principles and a style that has proven not only to be successful; it will take you to a "best-in-class" status for the organization and the people in it. You will be respected by your associates and recognized as a manager with a promising future for an eventual leadership position by utilizing this model.

QUALITY SHOULD BE INTEGRATED INTO ALL PARTS OF YOUR ORGANIZATION

The simplified versions of the definition for quality are "meeting and exceeding the expectations of the customers," or "doing the right things right, at the right time." This will leave you with two obvious questions. How can my organization grow if we spend all our time on existing customers? What about the need to work on developing potential customers as well? Both are important because perceived quality and value are directly related to increased market share as well as retaining existing customers. When manufacturers listen only to their existing customers, they will not hear the voices of those who have good reason to buy elsewhere. Thus, every organization must have a strong marketing and research team. As an effective manager you will need to know why the competition's customers buy elsewhere. You will need to convince some share of these potential customers that your organization's products and services are better.

Your organization will be comprised of many and critical processes. These improvements do not simply happen; the organizational culture makes it happen. When quality is defined as what the customers expect and need and is considered in every process, management is able to completely redirect its focus from the bottom line. This quality is not solely based on appearance and financial success.

THREE IMPORTANT EXPECTATION SETS

All of the critical processes established and monitored in the organization and all the changes made to improve quality are done to serve your customers better. The process of managing and continuously improving quality takes place within three broad sets of expectations in any organization. These three sets of expectations are internal customers' expectations, external customers' expectations, and owners'/investors' expectations. The ongoing identification, monitoring, and balancing of these expectations become central to the mission of your organization. Focus on these and you will be successful.

The best organizations place customers first, starting with the internal customers, and then concentrating on the external customers. The needs and expectations of these two groups are the driving force behind your vision, mission, and values. Internal customers (associates) must take care of external customers (those who purchase the products and services) so your goals can be met. The quality perceived by external customers determines the level of improvement needed in products and services, so it is essential to monitor and evaluate all external customer feedback. So, you must listen attentively to feedback from both sets of customers.

EXPECTATIONS IN DECISION MAKING

The three sets of expectations must be considered and balanced when making all decisions in the organization. In other words, a decision cannot be made that favors the external customer at the expense of the internal customer. Also, decisions cannot be made that favor both internal and external customers, but will be detrimental to your organization's financial performance. Again, all three sets of expectations must be balanced in the process of managing change. Also, when making decisions, review your options as if you were one or two levels higher in the organization structure. Options will look different at that vantage point, and your decision might change.

CUSTOMER-DRIVEN ORGANIZATIONS

Quality-driven organizations are customer-driven organizations, but how can customers be the driving force behind everything an organization does? This is best understood if we look at this in reverse. Examine your organization, whose policies, processes, and general methods of doing business are based entirely your thinking. You do not want to be responsible for an organization that will alienate and lose its customers and eventually cease to exist.

Successful organizations listen to their customers. We refer to this as "listening to the voices of quality" or "the pathway to continuous improvement." If everyone is involved in the process, there will be more ideas from which to choose.

When a customer provides feedback to you regarding implementing a change in your services, recognize their contribution, because this will strengthen the partnership. This is an example of involving your customers in the process; they have the opportunity for partnering and creating opportunities for change and growth.

INTERNAL CUSTOMER TEAMS

How can you take your organization to a level separate and higher than that of the growing list of competitors? As an effective manager, you must recognize that the organization's success is not simply a direct result of effective leadership. Rather, it is the combined efforts of all associates, managers, and leaders. Leaders, management, and associates become interdependent because of this; they rely on each other with the mutual goal of continuous improvement. This emphasizes the importance of getting everyone involved in the decision-making process.

ASSOCIATES FIRST OR EXTERNAL CUSTOMERS FIRST?

Initially, you must implement an associate-first orientation. Everything you do must be based on satisfying the needs and meeting the expectations of your associates. You need to communicate with them and listen to their concerns and ideas. By communicating with them and listening to them, you will build trust and a lasting partnership that works toward reducing associate turnover, which in turn will enhance continuous improvement of services and products and associate morale.

As Patrick Mene from The Ritz-Carlton Hotel Company once advised us: "Involve associates in the planning of the work that affects them, to increase the pride and joy they derive from their work." The goal is to develop a strategic alliance between the organization and its associate team. Always remember that your associates are more than employees, they are your customers and must be served by you as a manager.

The more you know about your associates' needs and expectations, the better able you are to give them the support, tools, ideas, and recognition they desire and deserve. In turn, the more successful your associates are because they know that you trust and believe in them, the higher the external customer satisfaction levels become.

You also need to gain insight into how and what your associates think and value. Knowing this enables you to be a better communicator. You will soon learn that all associates are different and the required level of support needed will vary.

At HDS Services our managers and leaders were encouraged to not go directly to their office upon arriving at work. Instead, they were encouraged to stop and talk with each of their associates before entering their office. This practice sent an "associates first" message as part of our culture to the entire staff at HDS Services. In some circles, this is also referred to as managing by walking around (MBWA). This practice builds trust and removes fear from the relationship between you and the associates.

Your recognition of your associate's success is also very effective in retention, because it reinforces and improves the contribution of the associates. Recognition does not have to wait for the awards banquet or annual evaluation. It can be done on a daily basis, and it is particularly effective when taking place in the presence of peers. These daily kudos and suggestions help make your associates' day.

Associates who are committed to the organization's vision, mission, and values can be a powerful source of energy. So you should remember to connect your associates to the decision-making process.

EXTERNAL CUSTOMERS

The steps involved in improving external customer satisfaction are the same as those of associates. First, you must identify who your external customers are. You need to know what they need, want, and expect. You must exceed what is expected and add extras. Extras could be product features that the external customer did not expect initially or experiences that make the encounter with the organization's associates memorable.

Today, most effective managers promise and deliver superior customer service. In fact, with the progressive expectations of today's increasingly sophisticated customers, the minimum levels of service expected have been increasing. Additionally, today's external customers are more attuned to price and believe that the lower the price, the better the value.

Furthermore, many of your customers view products as indistinguishable commodities. What they can purchase from you can and will be purchased from the competition. A lower price will deliver more value for the same product. Remember that higher levels of service also add value.

Your organization must realize that there is a difference between quality that meets expectations and quality that exceeds expectations. Today, intangible aspects of customer service are growing more important than the tangible aspects. Tangible aspects of quality relate to technical elements. The intangible parts of service are more difficult to create, deliver, and measure because they are the personal side of the transaction. The smile by the person working behind the counter is an intangible service element. These intangibles make the service experience memorable.

Customers who are totally satisfied by both tangible and intangible parts of service truly love the organization and are more likely to become loyal customers. Customers who love the product or service, and consequently your organization, have a vested interest in building the relationship. They are not likely to defect on price alone.

WELCOMING CUSTOMER COMPLAINTS

Yesterday's managers were satisfied when they heard no complaints. The assumption was that everything was going right. Now we know that often this is not the case. You will have to make it easier for customers to complain if you want valuable feedback. You need to roll out the red carpet for complaints.

These complaints must be shared with associates and associate teams that are empowered.

Empowerment minimizes your follow-up because it assists in making associates more responsible for their actions. Empowerment is simply providing direction for what needs to be done, the tools to do it, and then getting out of the way so people can achieve the results.

When associates have the power to fix problems there is no need for management to "fix the blame."

If all associates believe in and align with the organization's values, vision, and mission, they will be empowered to make well-informed decisions. Associates must be able to make decisions without fear of failure.

Trust is by far the most important pillar of empowerment because it is all-encompassing. Trust works both ways, with associates knowing and feeling comfortable that they have your total support. Trust extends beyond comfort and confidence. It involves caring for others as well.

Constructing Your Team

Self-directed teams will work with little supervision or direction from you. These teams are empowered to resolve issues and decide on the best course of action. Teams should be diverse and utilize synergy, and each individual must value the differences in people and strongly respect their teammates.

Steps in the Decision-Making Process

Oren Harari quotes Colin Powell on the correct timing of making decisions: "Don't wait until it is too late. Too much fact gathering leads to analysis-paralysis. When you have 40% to 70% of the information, go with your gut. Reducing risk really increases risk." At HDS Services, our standard decision-making process used five steps. Initially, feedback was gathered from internal and external customers. The feedback included hassles, issues, ideas, and suggestions.

Step One: Gaining Feedback
The initial step in the decision-making process relates to getting feedback. The question is how do we know which item to select first, and how do we get the ideas and issues? Ideas are suggestions that surface as part of the organization's endeavor to use suggestions to continuously improve. Issues are identified through the dehassling process. This leads us to the most commonly utilized tool, which is brainstorming.

Step Two: Brainstorming Hassles
Teams of associates meet to discuss those items that present barriers in making improvements to products, services, and key processes. A facilitator is chosen to chair the meeting, and he or she asks the members of the group to present their burning issues. Most issues relate to things done wrong, doing things over again, or frustrations. These hassles are documented and posted around the room where everyone can review the results of their brainstorming. When the session has been completed, the facilitator requests that each individual review all items. Then, the

items are listed in order of their individual priority or significance. This completes the second step in the decision-making process.

Step Three: Prioritizing the Root Causes

Smaller teams are assigned to work on the various issues and ideas, so that as many as possible are addressed simultaneously. The initial step is to identify the root causes of the chosen issues and ideas. They will brainstorm the root causes and develop a list for prioritizing. Once prioritized, the team will know where to start the action process.

Step Four: Develop Workable Solutions and Action Plan

The group now reviews each root cause and develops workable solutions to formulate an effective action plan. Several root causes are addressed simultaneously. Through idea generation among the group, interventions are discussed and plans are made for implementation. The interventions are put into practice, and the effect of the change is monitored.

Step Five: Monitor for Effectiveness

Once in progress, the results of the process are monitored by measuring their effectiveness. If the intervention is effective and productive, it must become part of the organization's strategic business plan to improve.

As all the issues and ideas are addressed; the continuous improvement CI process begins. This process must be thought of as a journey, because the changes that shift the organization's culture will take three to five years to achieve significant shifts in paradigms.

> At HDS Services, we used the principles in their basic form and simply avoided most technical aspects. The organization's culture was unique and mirrored that of managing for quality.

MANAGEMENT'S ROLE

In your role as a manager, make it a top priority to learn the organization's vision, mission, and core values, and get on board fast.

Remember to:

- Get everyone involved
- Encourage and welcome associates' input

- Promote bottom-up idea flow
- Manage by walking around
- Mentor your associates and find your mentor
- Look for the person you respect the most, because that is the person from whom you learn the most
- Finish the plan
- Dress for success (the next position)
- Network—be seen and heard
- Be aggressive but humble as well
- Make the tough decisions because favoring mediocrity leads to your best performers being unhappy and ultimately leaving

THE VANO MANAGER

Patrick Mene of the Ritz-Carlton Hotel Company was the vice president of quality when the company won the Malcolm Baldrige National Quality Award twice. He shared with us that there are two different types of managers: the Ritz-Carlton manager and the VANO (visual appearance/accounting numbers only) manager.

The VANO manager believes:

1. A sales transaction is just a number.
2. The level of internal and external customer satisfaction does not impact profit.
3. Quality is solely the visual appearance of the facility.
4. Profit is the difference between sales and cost.
5. Today's profit is the primary objective, no matter what.

The Ritz-Carlton manager, on the other hand, believes there is a need to produce a work environment that:

1. Helps people live better
2. Treats people with dignity
3. Involves people in the planning of the work that affects them, to increase the pride and joy they derive from their work

Another company that has excelled in its performance and growth in recent years is Starbucks. Their growth has accelerated because of intense customer loyalty and leadership's continued strong commitment to associate motivation, excellence in customer service and satisfaction, and community involvement. Some of the factors driving their success are experiencing forty million customer visits each week, an associate turnover rate that is 250 percent lower than the industry standard, and successfully opening five new stores each day. At the company's foundation are five core principles that continue to separate Starbucks from the many other operators in the coffeehouse industry.

One: Make It Your Own
Partners (associates) think about customer service in a way that allows each one of them to connect with customers personally. According to Chairman Howard Schultz, "We are not in the coffee business serving people; we are in the service business serving coffee."

Two: Everything Matters
Paying attention to every detail gives Starbucks a competitive advantage because it builds loyalty, as managers put themselves in the shoes of the customers.

Three: Surprise and Delight
Starbucks delivers consistent product and service quality to delight customers. Associates seek ways to surprise and engage customers.

Four: Embrace Resistance
Starbucks receives many forms of resistance from communities, international organizations, and, at times, customers, but then uses the criticism to become better.

Five: Leave Your Mark
People want to do business with and work for conscientious organizations. Starbucks encourages its people to be involved with their communities, matching cash contributions.

> I personally am a raving fan of Starbucks. I am there most mornings and periodically in the afternoon as well, because I continue to be impressed with the overall experience, the consistency of personalized service, product quality, and innovative marketing. In addition, I have overheard Starbuck interviews while there as a customer, and their interview process is definitely very thorough and well planned.

CHAPTER SIX

REFERENCES

Abshire, David. "Trustworthy Leaders." *Leadership Excellence*, April 2007, 24 (4): 20.

Allen, Robin Lee. "Expert: Managers Must Set Example for Gen Y Kidployees." *Nation's Restaurant News*, October 2005, 39 (41): 54.

Armstrong, Lance, and Sally Jenkins. *It's not about the Bike; My Journey Back to Life*. New York: Putnam and Sons Publishing, 2000.

Giuliani, Rudolph. *Leadership*. New York: Miromax Books, 2002.

Harari, Oren. *The Leadership Secrets of Colin Powell*. New York: McGraw Hill, 2002.

King, John H., Jr., and Ronald F. Cichy. *Managing for Quality in the Hospitality Industry*. Upper Saddle River, NJ: Pearson Prentice Hall, 2006.

Michelli, Joseph. "Starbucks Experience." *Leadership Excellence*, November 2006, 23 (11): 10.

Powell, Colin L., and Joseph E. Persico. *My American Journey*. New York: Ballantine Books, 1996.

Chapter Seven
Leading With Emotional
Intelligence

The Emotionally Intelligent Leader

Colin Powell insisted that "his team have fun in their command. Do not always run at a breakneck pace. Take leave when you have earned it and spend time with your family."

"Surround yourself with people who take their work seriously, but not themselves. These are the people with balance in their lives who like to laugh and who have non-job priorities which they approach with the same passion they do their work," wrote Oren Harari in 1996.

Most associates prefer to work with leaders who know when to be commanding and when to approach situations more as facilitators and with understanding. Displaying understanding by the leader requires a higher level of emotional intelligence.

Managers and Leaders Use Emotional Intelligence

These are examples of leaders and managers with emotional intelligence. They keep their cool in emotionally heated situations and resolve issues in ways that are atypical to the individual who sees everything as black and white. This individual is not able to see performance outcomes and issues from an emotional viewpoint. The leader with emotional intelligence understands the behaviors of associates and is capable of improving the performance of individuals and the team by offering interventions or solutions that recognize the emotions involved in the decision-making process. The most effective leaders possess emotional intelligence and thoroughly understand people, their emotions, their capabilities, and basically how they do the things that they do, and why.

Emotional Intelligence (EI) is a set of abilities or capabilities that an individual utilizes to understand, perceive, and manage their emotions and others' emotions. Our EI model (Cichy, Cha, and Kim) was first tested and validated in 2005, then again validated in our phase II research in 2006. In 2006, we confirmed the three dimensions of EI: *IN, OUT,* and *RELATIONSHIPS.*

Before emotional intelligence (EI) became known as a fundamental tool in the effective leader's portfolio, we referred to these as "social skills" or "people skills." Leaders with emotional intelligence place a higher value on each of the organization's associates. They understand the associate development challenge and clearly know that development is the better choice when it comes to dealing with associate issues and challenges. The EI skills when put into practice not only resolve the immediate issues, they provide a learning experience for all parties involved. Thus, there are long-term positive consequences and results. These skills include both intrapersonal, relating to being self-smart, and interpersonal, which was being people smart (relating to others). Unlike the intelligent quotient (IQ), which involves analytical intelligence and the ability to solve mathematic and verbal problems, emotional intelligence is being capable of resolving associates' issues by walking through the root causes of these issues from a fundamental emotional viewpoint. It is not what happened or how it happened. It is a consideration of the feelings of each and their impact on why it happened. Knowing the associates' emotional tendencies allows the leader to better resolve issues without taking more drastic, punitive, ineffective actions. This supports the organization's responsibility by encouraging the organization's intellectual capital.

Emotional intelligence allows managers to resolve problems on a counseling/learning basis, rather than "this is the way I see things, and you need to do or change this or else." This does not mean that everything must be negotiated each time. Rather, it means that discussions with associates must begin with an understanding of each others' feelings and include your requests for input and ideas, information from the leader that is unknown to the associate, and attentive listening by both parties until resolution is reached. Remember that your role as a leader includes directing changes in the organization. You should know about associates' emotions and values, because these will affect how the proposed changes are developed and implemented. You want the changes to be received in a positive way. Resistance will come with most changes, so your sensitivity to associates' emotions is critical.

EI, SELF-ESTEEM, AND TEMPER

We also find that emotions can be regulated over time through learning about self and others. We will never remove the emotional makeup of people, others and ourselves, from our roles as leaders. However, through meaningful conversations and mentoring, the leader can achieve positive, productive change in individuals on their team. Some of the more common emotional outcomes are self-esteem and temper. Each of us has likely had personal experience with dealing with associates in both managerial and leadership positions with personality traits reflecting low self-esteem, unwarranted high self-esteem, and the inability to control one's temper. Sometimes we as leaders fall into acting the same way or responding to another acting that way with the same behavior.

Once all understand that there is no place for tantrums in the work environment, they realize it is time to do something about their situation. Once the behavior is recognized by people in the organization, they need to understand that the organization has the desire to assist them in correcting the problem. Obviously, counseling in anger management is the correct path to resolution. Leadership or management must deal with this issue head-on but in a professional, caring manner. Controlling anger can be achieved in almost all cases. So, you should recognize that there is a major upside to resolving the anger issue and retaining the valued associate.

A situation with self-esteem is more difficult to deal with, especially if the person is in a leadership role. Low self-esteem produces fear, poor and erratic decision making, a negative attitude, associate disrespect, and a total breakdown in the management of this person's area of responsibility. Trying to build this individual's self-confidence is the obvious goal of organization leadership, but it is seldom achieved. Mentoring, support, and coaching are necessary elements of success in changing this associate. What happens in most cases is the person takes the position that he or she is the boss, based solely on title and position in the organization. Once this position surfaces, the entire associate relationship foundation falls apart. How does one with low self-esteem reach such a high level in the organization? In most cases, it is through friendship and past experiences taking precedent over ability and possessing the qualities, keys, and secrets of an effective leader.

Emotional intelligence becomes a very powerful predictor of others' behavior, reactions to mentoring and counseling, and personal behavior related to future change. This is an asset possessed by CEOs, who must successfully determine how to take the team on the leadership journey to reach their vision. The journey always involves change, and knowing how others will handle change is a key ingredient in goal achievement. One of the main roles of the leader is that of facilitator, that is, the capability to guide members of the team through change. So, emotional intelligence can make the difference between good and poor leaders, and this is strongly linked to effective leadership. Again, management positions demand strong technical skills, and leadership roles require both a strong managerial skills portfolio as well as emotional intelligence.

A new emotional intelligence framework was tested for validity and determined to be reliable by Cichy, Cha, and Kim (2005). Further studies of private club industry chief operating officers (COOs) and general managers were conducted in 2006, 2007, 2008, and 2009. The key dimensions of *in*, *out*, and *relationships* were discovered and reinforced. *IN* is the ability to sense, lead, and utilize one's own emotions. *OUT* is the ability to be aware of, relate to, and understand others' emotions. *RELATIONSHIPS* is the ability to integrate your emotional experiences with your own thoughts and actions while interacting with others. The top results, based on ranking, are presented in Table 1.

Table 1 – IN, OUT, RELATIONSHIPS–Top EI Results

Top Ranked Item	Mean
IN Ability/Capability I am able to sense my own feelings.	4.13
OUT Ability/Capability I am sensitive to other people's emotions.	4.06
RELATIONSHIPS Ability/Capability People would say I am a cooperative, contributing, and a positive team member.	4.45

Numbers in the mean column indicate means based on the scale from 1 = very seldom or not true of me, to 5 = very often or true of me.

IN, OUT, RELATIONSHIPS

The top *IN*, *OUT*, and *RELATIONSHIPS* result for each dimension is presented in Table 1. In each dimension, the top item is listed based on a ranking by averages (indicated in parentheses) of all items in that dimension. The *IN* dimension has eight items; the *OUT* dimension has seven items; and the *RELATIONSHIPS* dimension has five items. In other words, there are twenty total items in our three-dimension model; we are only showing the top ranked item in each of the three dimensions.

The top-ranked *IN* ability is: "I am able to sense my own feelings." Knowing yourself and having the ability to sense your own emotions relates to our earlier research discoveries that leadership is first, foremost, and always an inner quest. It is important to remain true to yourself by being in touch regularly with your feelings. Your feelings are an insight into your values and your purpose. When a leader's values are aligned with those of the organization, it is easier to be effective as a leader of that organization. One respondent advised: "Be true to yourself. Do not let a change in your surroundings change your own personal belief structure." Another wrote: "Create your own identity and personality and be sure to find a club that is consistent with your ideas."

The *IN* capability of sensing your own feelings comes with knowing yourself, and having the ability to accurately be in touch with your own emotions to help you be more effective. This is especially important when matching personal values to those of your organization. Be true to yourself. Do not let a change in your surroundings change your own personal belief structure. Create your own identity and personality, and be sure to find an organization that is consistent with your ideas. Self-integrity is the manager's most important attribute. Remain true to yourself; do not let the culture of the organization overshadow your personal values and beliefs. The right position needs to be the right fit; your values need to match the organization's values.

The top ranked *OUT* capability is: "I am sensitive to other people's emotions." How does a leader show sensitivity? First, by listening to others and trying to connect with the other person's feelings as they perceive them. Second, by being fair to others and treating them with respect. One respondent wrote that a leader must "be fair to everyone, all the time: associates, external customers (called members in a private club), suppliers, family, and friends." Sensitivity also is observable when the leader understands the balance of associate satisfaction and customer satisfaction.

Understanding and appreciating emotions of others are essential leadership skills. It is critical that you understand and appreciate how you impact others' emotions. As you transition into a leadership role, always recognize the effect your position has on the people who work with you. Be fair and understanding to your associates and other colleagues and work to make them better people, and it will reflect positively to others. Leaders believe that their organization is what they make of it, much like any other organization. The opportunity to make impacts on others is large.

The top ranked **RELATIONSHIPS** capability is: "People would say I am a cooperative, contributing, and a positive team member." Associates in an organization look to the managers and leaders to be the champions of cooperation through leading the way. Effective leaders are cooperative and usually are optimistic. It is through these actions that they contribute to the development of others and to moving the organization forward. Positive, meaningful dialogue with others allows them to see the manager or leader as someone who they can rely on and trust. One participant wrote that you must "say what you mean and mean what you say. Be consistent in your habits and practices and lead by example. Never ask anyone in your organization to do something that you would not be prepared to do yourself."

In order to be a positive, cooperative, and contributing team member, many managers and leaders follow the mantra of leading by example. One leader summed up this ability by saying: "Don't be a dictator; eventually it will lead to anarchy. A great leader not only leads but gets down in the trenches beside them. Treat your staff as if no job is below you and show them you respect their position." Leaders need to say what they mean and mean what they say.

Because they practice this ability each day, leaders can easily build and participate in mutually satisfying relationships characterized by openness and affection. Some interpret this as compassion, while others view it as development of people in the organization. A leader must learn to have compassion with all in the organization and understand that they all have something to contribute to the success of the organization. Take care of your associates; they are the lifeblood of the organization. The key to your success as a leader is your associates. Develop their skills, diversify, support, and encourage teamwork among all in the organization. Depend on each other and benefit from its success. As a leader, you are only as good as the people you have working around you.

Leaders practice identifying problems and developing and putting into place effective solutions. To effectively deal with conflict in relationships with others, managers and leaders quickly resolve the problem by first seeking input from those involved. They do not take complaints personally and do not waste time on issues out of their control. These leaders look at the "real issues" and don't focus on the things they cannot control. They are persistent.

Knowing one's self and others (both personally and with the organization) is important, but knowing how to relate and manage feelings and relationships is also what separates managers from effective leaders. Thus, emotional intelligence is directly linked to effective leadership and a successful, winning organization. Poor leaders either are unaware of their feelings and others' feelings, or are incapable of putting the two together to build relationships.

On the other end of the poor leader spectrum is the leader who uses others' feelings to dominate decision making and developmental processes.

The best leaders are emotionally adept at coaching and work to continuously improve this strength. They not only lead with emotional intelligence, but they teach it to their associates to build the associates' leadership capabilities. Developing relationships takes a positive attitude, and with continued practice, you become more effective. Use the feelings and emotions of others to learn something new, and recognize that possessing this set of emotional intelligence skills is often much more important than operational skills and knowledge.

The results of the studies by Cichy, Cha, and Kim produced the following suggestions regarding how to be a more effective leader.

1. Measure the success of the organization by the success of others.

2. Get ideas, input, and criticism from others, and be a great listener (talk only 25 percent of the time). Remember to be empathetic and see the entire situation from the other person's point of view. Empathy demonstrates to the other person that you care, are genuine, and will respond to concerns.

3. When listening to the associate, it is vital to not simply hear the words, but to try to understand the real meaning of the message. By listening carefully and showing you are eager to understand the real message, you will encourage others to open up and clarify their true meaning. Active listening requires that you "be there" and ask questions.

4. Recognize that relationships are a two-way street and that mutual trust is the backbone of a strong relationship. Being candid and honest in your discussions will greatly enhance the results.

5. Show compassion when dealing with emotions of others. Associates can immediately sense compassion and are more likely to trust the superior.

6. Build relationships with customers, peers, associates (all), and suppliers. Do not be wary of developing long-term partnerships, and remember that reaching your vision is a journey.

A related "Leadership Lesson from the Eagle" states: "The best leaders are excellent listeners, which is one of the cornerstones of leadership. Careful listening leads to hearing and understanding what is not being said."

First Three Pillars of EI:

Knowing Self, Knowing Others, Building Relationships

We have discussed three of the five pillars of emotional intelligence. These three are awareness of self and leading self, understanding and knowing others, and building and using relationships. Knowing one's self comes first, because without it we will never understand others. If we know ourselves, we will not take the wrong position in a wrong organization, and we will not enter into a relationship that is counterproductive or negative. Also, knowing self gives us the confidence to help others because we will know how to take the appropriate action.

Knowing others gives you the inside track on empowering others to motivate themselves. You will know exactly how to deal with the situation at hand because you can anticipate their reaction. This not only allows you to get where you want to be with the individual, it accelerates success.

Building relationships is all about interaction with others. We know we can help them manage their feelings to the benefit of the organization, not to our own individual personal success. Positive relationships with your people lead to strong teamwork and the achievement of goals.

Fourth and Fifth Pillars of EI:

Self-Control and Patience

The fourth pillar is having self-control. We must not show anger or use emotional outbursts. Others want to work with those individuals that show professionalism and are rational thinkers. When we control our emotions, we are better leaders and managers in stressful situations. It will raise the level of respect others have for us, and they will be more likely to use us as a role model.

The fifth pillar is showing patience and compassion when dealing with others. When we listen we understand the feelings of others. But, we also must see the situation through the eyes of others. Remember, there are many sides and perspectives of each and every situation. Trust plays a major role in our seeing the situation through the eyes of others. We know that lasting trust is earned. But, there is also an element of trust or the opposite when we first meet someone. It is like the sixth sense that successful leaders possess. We immediately connect with people who listen to us and demonstrate sensitivity, concern, or interest. Individuals who lack this compassion are obviously concerned only about themselves and ignore others. They seldom connect with others.

COMPARING HIGH AND LOW EI GROUPS

After we had collected the EI results, we split the respondents into two groups—high EI and low EI—based on the median (i.e., the middle value) of the total EI scores. Our goal was to then examine the social skills and stress management skills of the two groups, based on additional questions included in our survey.

Social Skills

The roots of Emotional Intelligence go back to 1920 when social intelligence was defined as a person's ability to "act wisely in human relations." **Social skills**, on the other hand, are related to your ability to clearly express your own ideas, opinions, and thoughts to others, sense the emotions and motivations of others, and have others respond in desirable and effective ways. Social skills include the skills of what and how you communicate, your sensitivity to the feelings and drivers of others, and the outcomes of the interactions.

We measured participants' social skills using five questions in our survey and discovered that there was a very high correlation between EI and social skills. Further, those in the high EI group were better at recognizing (and presumably practicing) social skills than those in the low EI group.

One participant said: "Constantly work at building relationships with all levels of staff and teammates. Meaning positive, meaningful dialogue that allows your staff to see you as someone they can rely on, but also respect as a leader/coach." Another wrote: "Be visible and friendly to both your members and staff, and get in the trenches with your employees." You cannot manage an organization from your office. And a third perhaps summed it up best when noting that "people will often forget what you told them. They will seldom remember what you did for them, but they will always remember how you treated them. Treat people well."

Stress Management Skills

Of all the EI competencies, **stress management** may be the most visible. In our study, stress management was assessed using five items, and focused on the development of constructive solutions for frustrations, management of highly demanding workloads, acting professional, and being a calming influence for associates and others. Stress management was targeted to the ability to manage stress in the workplace, not necessarily personal stress management, although the two are usually related.

After measuring participants' stress management skills using five questions in our survey, we discovered that there was a high correlation between EI and stress management. Further, those in the high EI group were better at managing stress than those in the low EI group.

One leader advised: "think before you act and don't be afraid to reach out to people you respect to seek advice. Learn from your own mistakes and those of others." Another wrote: "Look at the 'real issues' and don't focus on the things you cannot control. Be persistent." And a third pointed out, "It is a tough business, but it has its rewards. Stay true to yourself; keep up with your continuing education, trends, and perfecting your skills."

What Does This Mean for You as an Emerging Leader?

A number of our findings give insights into a set of required skills to be an effective emerging leader. Certainly, Emotional Intelligence capabilities are essential in organizations, since there is such a heavy reliance on building and strengthening long-term relationships. Both internal and external customers not only expect satisfying relationships in the organizations they choose to support or work in; in many respects, this is what they are paying (either with their time or money) to experience.

Social skills are critical for the emerging leader and the development of these skills is enhanced when the individual builds EI abilities. The two skill sets are highly correlated. Some chose careers with certain organizations because these organizations provide a venue in which to develop and demonstrate their own social skills. Social skills are related to your ability to clearly express yourself, feel where others are "coming from," and achieve desirable and effective results from these interactions.

Stress management is all about how you react to the inevitable demands, frustrations, and pressures that you and others experience in your organization. When the response is calming and settling for others, focused on getting done what needs to be done, and the identification of constructive solutions for what at first pass seemed overwhelming, you are on your way to successfully managing workplace stress. Our study suggests that those who have higher EI are more capable of managing stress.

Real Examples of EI

At HDS Services, being focused on customer and client expectations and their emotional responses was of particular importance. In the hospitality business, we need to read between the lines when discussing business with a client. Even in dealing with a long-term client partner, situations will surface that test the relationship. We will need to draw from our knowledge about that client and their emotions. At HDS, our success rate in these situations was close to 100 percent. The toughest challenges were more likely to surface when encountering a new client executive. I remember meeting for the first time with a new administrator of a facility that was a long-term partner. Our vice president of marketing joined me. Unfortunately, this new client was totally adverse to outsourcing services. His position was based on perceptions of other organizations in our industry and even more on his desire to personally control the management of all departments in his facility.

My colleague and I were literally asked to leave his office during the meeting. We were able to schedule another meeting with this individual, who finally began to listen to our strategic plan for services to his facility. We worked our way through achievement of many goals during that first year. Much of our success was achieved through learning his emotional state and getting to know him. Eventually, this client became a better partner. At the time he retired from that facility, he was actually a friend. The lesson learned in this case was that no matter how difficult the initial challenge is, you can succeed by getting to know others' emotions and feelings, and using these in developing your plan to succeed.

In this case we knew ourselves and the services which we provided to make the client's organization a success. We knew this because our leadership team made it a practice to progressively measure our assets and to know self. This, along with our managing for quality culture, provided us with the qualities, keys, and secrets to be successful. Dealing with this challenging client was a great learning experience because we gained insight from an external customer about his paradigm and how to build a relationship by knowing self and the client. Would other organizations be able to succeed in this situation? We cannot directly answer this question, but the most common fatal flaws of leadership are well known.

Fatal flaws of leadership were presented by Sidney Finkelstein in his article "The Seven Habits of Spectacularly Unsuccessful Executives." We believe the predominant leadership flaws involve thinking they have all the answers, thus driving the good and talented people out of the organization and always relying on what has worked in the past which produces gridlock and eventual corporate failure. Successful companies have leaders who accept and drive change, and surround themselves with talent.

According to Finkelstein, these are powerful reminders of how leaders are not only responsible for growth but are sometimes the architects of failure. Leaders must be vigilant in all aspects of their leadership responsibilities.

Using the lessons learned from emotional intelligence, we are now in a better position to continue our emerging leadership journeys.

Chapter Seven

References

Cichy, Ronald F., James B. Singerling, J. M. Cha, and S. H. Kim. "The Emotional Intelligence of Private Club Leaders." *Club Management*, August 2005, 84 (4): 38–40.

Cichy, Ronald F., and James B. Singerling. "Emotional Intelligence and Leadership—Validating a New EI Scale." *Club Managers Association of America 79th Annual Educational Proceedings Manual*, 2006.

Cichy, Ronald F., James B. Singerling, J. M. Cha, and S. H. Kim. "Emotional Intelligence and Your Feelings about Your Volunteer Board Leadership in Your Club." *The Boardroom*, July/August 2006, 10:26, 28, 74.

Cichy, Ronald F., J. M. Cha, and S. H. Kim. "Private Club Leaders' Emotional Intelligence: Development and Validation of a New Measure of Emotional Intelligence." *Journal of Hospitality & Tourism Research*, February 2007, 31 (1): 39–55.

Harari, Oren. *The Leadership Secrets of Colin Powell.* New York: McGraw Hill, 2002.

Finkelstein, Sidney. "The Seven Habits of Spectacularly Unsuccessful Executives." *Ivey Business Journal*, January/February 2004, 1–6.

Chapter Eight
Planning and Building
Your Career

Managing Your Career Progression

Having now learned who you are and what kind of manager and leader you are or are likely to be, we next will take a look at how you can best manage your journey from the beginning to that of being a leader. First, you must understand how many career progression steps there are in your particular leadership journey. Each organization is different. Some could have as few as three management steps to a leadership position, while others could have many more. Once you identify these steps in your particular situation, you will be able to strategically plan your journey and the approximate timetable to become a leader. Action steps will be clearly identified as well. Your attitude will play a major role in how you succeed at each step in this journey.

For the manager or leader, perpetual optimism is a force multiplier. Unfortunately, pessimism and cynicism are also force multipliers. Positive thinkers tend to push change to gain continuous improvement, because they do not fear the challenges associated with change. They actually embrace them. All effective leaders possess a strong, positive attitude. These positive thinkers push the "we can be the best" goal, without concern of not reaching it. Continuous improvement is a journey, and the goals continuously escalate to a higher level.

According to Michael Crom, executive vice president of Dale Carnegie Training, "students entering the business world need to:

1)   Accept themselves as they are, while focusing on the positives. And, use their strengths to their advantage.

2) Appreciate and respect yourself, and focus on your past achievements and success. This builds confidence.

3) Approach new experiences as opportunities, and do not be afraid to take some risks. This will build your self esteem.

4) Just be yourself. You are unique and people will be drawn to you. Subsequently, your feeling of self worth will improve.

5) Create a support system, because when you are down on yourself, you will have a support team to make you feel good about yourself." Being positive and confident provides the foundation for effective management and world-class leadership.

Another "Leadership Lesson from the Eagle" is applicable to perpetual optimism. "To be predictably known as the best is every leader's vision. But, your organization should never become predictable from a strategic point of view. Change will be driven by your actions, but never sacrifice your values for change."

DEVELOPING POWER THROUGH ATTITUDE

All of us learn our values and beliefs from our families, culture, and past experiences. The key to being successful in the leaders' career progression is the way we control or lack control over each step of the way. Let us refer to these choices as powerful (control) and powerless (lack control). The powerful individual is most likely from a family that focused on hard work, education, and being responsible. The powerless person most likely came from a family that believed there was little control over life, in general, or one's career, in particular.

The powerless believe outside forces control their destiny and are likely to wait for something beyond their control to solve their problems. The powerful see themselves as responsible for solving their problems, and do so quickly. They do not wait for someone else to solve their problems for them. The powerful believe their skills and hard work will determine whether or not they get the promotion. They believe there are choices in life; therefore, they will more than likely have high self-esteem, exude confidence, and be assertive in moving toward a leadership position. Basically, this person is much happier, unencumbered, and more satisfied with his or her life. This leader also experiences less stress and thus has better health, which leads to longer leadership tenure.

How does one go about changing from a powerless person to one of high self-esteem who is in control of their own leadership journey? First, you need to know that anything worth doing begins with a dream or personal vision based on personal values. Also, you must understand that success in life, and especially transitioning to be a leader, does not just happen. It happens because you plan, set SMART goals, and take action to make them happen. SMART goals are Specific, Measurable, Attainable, Realistically high, and Timely. This method of managing your life results from having a positive attitude. It is important to know that attitudes, either positive or negative, are your habits of thought. The key word here is habit, because as we proceed in the journey, experiences will impact us and form opinions. Hopefully these experiences turn into positive discoveries, and if we respectively deal with these in the proper positive manner, our attitude will be positive and powerful. This is what you need to become: assertive, effective, and noticed in your organization.

Many of our CEO friends told us over the years that the majority of managers who never become leaders had an attitude problem, primarily indifference. Most of these people had the skills to succeed.

There are many people who tend to think about what is going to go wrong and how they might fail. They could use a positive attitude and think what is going to go right and precisely how they will succeed. To reiterate, much of the negative thinking comes from conditioning in early life, such as:

- How many can you finish?
- Children should be seen and go where you are not.
- Speak only when spoken to.

Here are some more helpful hints for being a successful manager and being recognized as having leadership potential.

- Understand that your behavior has a dramatic impact on peers and associates. Maintain a positive attitude, keep your cool, and be empathetic.
- Deliver 100 percent on your promises.
- Build trust so associates and customers can rely on you and respect you. Generally, be a nice person who cares about people.
- Be assertive in your roles in supervision and management so that you are noticed and recognized as a potential leader. Engage in discussions with your leader(s) several times each year regarding where you are in achieving your goals for succession, and what you can do to possibly accelerate a career move.
- Get involved with projects that will help you learn more about leadership.

- Attend all of the organization's social functions and demonstrate your ability to mingle, network, and manage any organizational politics.

- Do everything possible to help associates succeed. *Your success depends on it!*

Planning and Action

While attitude plays a major role in your success or failure in the leadership journey, knowing precisely where you want to be as a leader and having a clear understanding of the many steps in the journey are keys for achieving your goals. Identifying the ultimate objective and working your way back to the present is referred to as "back planning." By contrast, starting with today and trying to identify each step in the journey without knowing where you are going is practically impossible.

We have already discussed the type of activity and learning at the student and managerial levels. Now it is time to present the leadership responsibilities, because this is obviously your ultimate goal (to be in a leadership position). When we look at the transition or journey in the big picture, we find the following model useful.

P	O	CEO			T	T	O
E	R				A	E	R
O	I		Leader/Officer		S	C	I
P	E				K	H	E
L	N					N	N
E	T		Upper Management		A	I	T
	A				N	C	A
	T		Midmanagement		D	A	T
	I					L	I
	O						O
	N		Supervision				N
			Associates				

The leadership journey begins with mostly all task-oriented responsibilities. When you enter the world of supervision or midmanagement, your responsibilities begin to shift to some people functions. Task orientation drastically declines at the top management level. And, as a leader, the responsibilities are totally people oriented. You are probably wondering why we teach leaders to be "hands on"? Isn't this more task oriented? Actually not! Our version of "hands on" relates to spending time with the associates, supervisors, and midmanagers, *not* doing their work. Taking an interest in what they do and listening to them is having the key to the CEO's office. You will go all of the way to a leadership position with this management style.

The following chart outlines the differences between the duties of managers and leaders. Remember that the leader has been an excellent manager, thus they are aware of the key managerial duties, and, as a leader, will take a more global approach.

CATEGORY	MANAGERS	LEADERS
General	Focus on things Do things right Plan Organize Direct Control Follow rules	Focus on people Do the right things Inspire Influence Motivate Build Shape organizations
Planning	Budgeting Set targets Detail steps	Devise strategy Set direction Create vision
Organization	Structure Job routines	People consensus Communication
Directing	Resolve issues Negotiate	Empower Be a cheerleader

Again a manager's duties basically relate to tasks, while the leader devotes most of his or her time and energy toward people. The manager or student should look down the road to the leadership position they desire and back plan from there to the present.

An example of a back planning exercise would include:

A. Master Position Outline

   Ultimate objective—officer/leadership position

Step 6:   Regional manager

Step 5:   District manager

Step 4:   Property manager/general manager

Step 3:   Assistant property manager

Step 2:   Department manager

Step 1:   Assistant manager/supervisor

Student/associate

B. Position Responsibilities
List these responsibilities for each position that is new to your portfolio of skills and capabilities, both task- and people-oriented.

C. Learning/mentoring plan
List the names of the people who will teach you new areas of responsibility and coach you. This would include one-on-one mentoring, spending time with management/associates learning specific departmental functions, or attending classes or executive development programs to learn more advanced leadership skills such as organizational financial management, human resources, or business law.

D. Plan timetable
To the best of your knowledge, assign times to the various positions. This will give you an idea of how long you think it will take you to get there. Share this with your mentor to get advice and opinions on your plan and timetable.

As you progress through the journey, modify the plan, because situations will take place that will either slow or accelerate progress. This plan will enhance your ability to be successful in crossing the bridge to the new position. You will know what to expect from your new leader and your team, and what they expect from you.

GENERATIONAL DIFFERENCES

When you cross the bridge from student or associate to supervisor, the first steps are crucial. You will need to gain everyone's respect. This was covered earlier, but we need to discuss dealing with generational differences and expectations. Knowing about each generation, and there are four in the current workforce, provides you with a better way to manage and inspire associates of all ages. It is the common experiences of each generation that drive attitudes, behaviors, and lifestyles of its members. Each generation has a different level of expectations, unique attitudes, and varying perspectives. Each of these has an influence on the management/associate relationship. So, you will need to understand each generation and build strong relationships that lead to cooperation and job satisfaction. If not, the differences can lead to communication breakdown, mistrust, and lack of teamwork, all of which create problems for associate retention and customer satisfaction.

According to Jennifer Deal in her article "Generational Differences," the so-called generational gap is largely a result of miscommunication and misunderstanding, fueled by insecurities and desires for clout. Leaders need to learn how to use that common ground to effectively work with, work for, attract, manage, retain, and develop associates of all generations. Here are ten intergenerational facts or truths:

1. All generations have similar values.
2. Everyone wants respect.
3. Leaders must be trustworthy.
4. All generations want credibility.
5. No one wants politics.
6. No one *really* likes change.
7. Loyalty is based on context, not generation.
8. Young associates are as easily retained as older associates.
9. Everyone wants to learn.
10. Almost everyone wants a coach.

The four generations in the workforce in the first decade of the 2000s are the Silent Generation, Baby Boomers, Gen X'ers, and Gen Y'ers (Millennials).

The Silent Generation are ages 60–80 and were raised during the Depression and World War II. As children, they were taught to be seen and not heard. Their values include honesty, hard work, and dedication. They are accustomed to a top-down management style and respect authority.

Baby Boomers are ages 40–59 and are often referred to as being self-serving. They were raised in times of a strong economy but much political upheaval, so they have little respect for leadership and are very individualistic. They work hard for long hours, and they expect the same from those who report to them. They are also very creative.

Gen X'ers are ages 27–39 and were generally raised when their mothers worked outside the home. This is why they tend to be independent and self-reliant. Along with raising the bar on life–work balance, they are technically smart, strategic, and do not like supervision. Unlike Boomers, many Gen X women have given up their careers for raising their children at home. They react positively to opportunities for growth.

Gen Y'ers are ages 26 and less. They thrive on spontaneously developed short-term goals and expect feedback on everything they do, however minor or mundane. They are more comfortable than other generations with ethnic diversity and have a strong sense of social responsibility.

When you are promoted to a leadership position, the majority of your associates will be Gen Y'ers. Therefore, we will present additional details concerning their characteristics and how to best meet their expectations. Dr. Tim Elmore, at GrowingLeaders.com and a facilitator for Growing Leaders, Inc., has conducted extensive research into what he refers to as "the strange, contradictory characteristics of generation Y (A Generation of Paradox)." He outlines seven obvious paradoxes, and what to do as a leader to best develop them to emerge as a good manager and leader.

1. **They are sheltered, yet pressured.** They have been sheltered by their parents but have been pressured more than any other generation to make the grade. You should simplify everything for them, help them slow down, and help them set goals.

2. **They are self-absorbed, yet generous.** They prepare each morning for the day ahead, and spend more money on themselves than other generations did. But, they give more time and financial support to others. You should give them options to participate in major causes and their community.

3. **They are isolated by technology, yet very social.** Most of the contact they have with other people is through technology, thus their people skills are poor. You will need to teach them communication skills and how to develop relationships with others.

4. **They have been protected, but are adventurous.** Their parents and educators have prepared them for more school, not the real world. You need to assist them with becoming drivers, not passengers of life.

5. **They are diverse, yet team oriented.** There are many differences between these individuals, and all too often when they feel ostracized by their peers, they tend to use violence. You should help them appreciate the strengths in others and how to use these when building an effective team.

6. **They are visionary, yet vacillating.** They have a focused vision but have a tendency to change in a heartbeat. They are undecided about the future. You should keep them focused and committed.

7. **They are high achievers, but also high maintenance.** They require lots of attention, are very naïve, and are convinced they will make the world a better place. You should give them constant feedback and recognize every achievement.

These Gen Y'ers will expect leadership to be 100 percent ethical, yet they admit to cheating on tests in school themselves. It is obvious they will need the best mentoring available.

Ron Alsop best describes this generation in *The Trophy Kids Grow Up: How the Millennial Generation Is Shaking up the Workplace.* There is one overriding perception of this generation, and that is their sometimes outlandish expectations. They want to shape their jobs to fit their lives rather than adapt their lives to the workplace.

Most generations have been considered to be spoiled in their youth by their predecessors, but this generation has a strong sense of entitlement. Their expectations include higher pay (74 percent), flexible work schedules (61 percent), a promotion within a year (56 percent), and more personal and vacation time (50 percent), according to a survey by CareerBuilder.com. They want to be a CEO, but they do not want to give up time with their family. Most of these expectations stem from feelings of superiority. They say "I deserve favors from others, and I know I have more natural talents than most." They believe they are hard-working and utilize tools to get the job done, but they do not want to work more than 40 hours per week. They want to wear comfortable clothes and want to be able to spice up the dull workday by listening to their iPods. And, lastly, if organizational America does not like what they do and how they think, it is just too bad.

They think the annual evaluation is not enough. They want loads of attention on a weekly basis. "This generation was raised with so much affirmation and positive reinforcement that they come into the workplace needy for more," says Subha Barry, managing director and head of global diversity and inclusion at Merrill Lynch & Co.

Smart managers will listen to their young associates' opinions and involve them in the decision-making process. What is ironic is that the grumbling baby boomer managers are the same indulgent parents who produced this generation.

In an article entitled "The Class of 2001" that appeared in the *Management Review* in December 1999 by an anonymous author, students were asked to identify what organizations will be like in the future. Here are some of their answers:

1. Work will be a distraction from life.

2. There will not be an office, and we will spend more time with family.

3. We will work independently and not on a team.

4. Increased responsibility will bring more freedom.

5. Markets will continue to be more global.

6. Environmental issues will become #1.

7. There will be more small organizations and few larger organizations because they are too difficult to manage.

8. There will be more technical support with less hands-on management and less customer contact.

The key to successfully managing the four generations as a team is by creating a culture of inclusion. Will Ruch, in his article "Full Engagement," suggests three action steps for greater engagement:

1. Understand your workforce, including skill sets, personalities, and perspectives on culture.

2. Build and maintain a balanced workforce through strategic recruiting and selection. Retention strategies must vary for the various generations.

3. Create a culture in your organization that accepts and values all associates. And include multigenerational associates in the strategic planning process.

Acceptance of a multigenerational workforce and teams result in a diverse approach to problem solving and planning.

BUILDING STRENGTHS AND KEY COMPETENCIES

As you progress from position to position through your management/ leadership journey plan, there are some characteristics that the potential leader must develop and demonstrate. Everyone has some weaknesses, but rather than devoting all of your time to correcting these, build on your strengths in the following key competency areas:

- Associate satisfaction
- Customer satisfaction
- Organization results
- Diversity

As Jim Trinka writes in the article "Great Leader": "You do not need to be a super hero to be identified as a great leader."

How do you build on your strengths or key competencies? Jim Trinka suggests that you focus on companion competencies to raise the perception of the potential leader's behavior related to other competencies. Technical credibility is a companion competency to organizational skills such as strategic planning, and interpersonal skills are linked to developing managers.

Key competencies vary between industries. In the hospitality field some research has been completed to identify the most important competencies. This topic is reported in an article from the *Cornell Hotel & Restaurant Administration Quarterly*, February 2000.

The following are the top ten competencies from this study involving over seven hundred participants.

1. Ethics and integrity
2. Awareness of customer needs
3. Time management
4. Commitment to quality
5. Speaking with impact
6. Teamwork orientation
7. Planning
8. Flexibility and adaptability

9. Managing stakeholders

10. Building networks

These competencies could be adapted to all industries and by educators to prepare emerging leaders for future leadership positions. They should also be utilized by human resources executives to create an effective recruiting and evaluation model.

As you build your strengths and key competencies you will need to know what the leader does on a routine basis versus what you do in a management position. The responsibilities of a student/associate and a manager have been previously described. The routine of a leader typically includes the following:

- As a general manager: strategic planning for the property; develop property financial plan; monitor performance (operational goals, sales goals, administrative goals, financial goals); evaluation of vision, mission, and values; facilitate executive group meetings; oversee multidepartment teams; assess quality efforts; and attend regional meetings.

- As a multiunit manager: develop general managers; strategic planning (property/region); develop regional financial plan; monitor regional financial performance; monitor regional quality initiatives; attend organizational meetings; serve organizational teams; and lead community projects.

- As an officer of the organization: develop regional managers; manage strategic plan; manage organizational expansion projects as an executive committee member; special projects facilitator (board directed); public relations–national; serve on the organization's finance committee.

ASSERTIVENESS

Now that we know what the key leadership competencies are, what our personal plan is for making the transition from manager to leader, and what the qualities, keys, and secrets are, we need to determine our personal mission or how to get there. We talked about networking, assertiveness, and getting noticed in general terms, but we did not discuss the details involved.

Assertiveness relates to taking control of your destiny and managing the process of advancement through learning. It is not meant to be dominant and running over those who get in your way. That is being overly aggressive, which is apparent when an individual dominates meetings with their behavior. And, for some reason, you are perceived as being a threat. However, do not be passive and wait for someone to recognize your talent. Select someone from the outset to be your mentor who can provide you with periodic progress reports.

Remember that the key to a successful leadership journey begins with the planning process. The opposite approach would be to select a college or a first career opportunity without giving these steps much thought or plan development. Remember, you know yourself and you know what the qualities, keys, and secrets of leadership are for you. With this knowledge you are able to better develop your mission statement and strategic plan. Once in place, you can begin to take action. To achieve alignment with actions and mission requires discipline to understand yourself and the achievement both you and your mentor perceive. Keep in mind that as you get older (in your twenties or thirties), you may have a family with expectations as well. This will require your further attention to achieving balance between career and personal goals. If you find your life is out of alignment with your skills, potential, and expectations, you will need to take further action to correct the issues. Success in most organizations is at least 75 percent driven by actions rather than planning. So your success with implementation is what matters most. Experience has taught that it is easier to align with the organization than it is with the personal side.

Remember, you are in control of your own destiny. Do not allow anyone else to be totally responsible for achieving success for your career journey. So, your potential as a leader becomes more of a goal that you have strategically developed. Again, this will require discipline, especially in the areas of developing relationships within the organization. Be careful not to send the wrong message of arrogance by driving a very expensive car or wearing a watch that costs equally as much as an automobile. You should also manage the way you will eventually lead by respecting others, being confident but humble, and leaving your ego at the door.

In keeping with the emerging leader's development of a strategic plan to meet or exceed the expectations of the organization's executives throughout the management career, we asked our students to brainstorm a list of criteria on which they believed that they would be judged as emerging leaders. Organization executives typically conduct a talent review once or twice a year to assure that they have a succession plan and bench strength as they expand the organization. The list of criteria was developed by the students as a guide for their future development. This is the list of student-developed talent review criteria:

Adaptable	Delegate/empower	Open mind
Advancement	Do the right things	Optimistic
Aggressive	Driven	Organized
Aligned visions	Energetic	Passionate
Ambitious	Ethical	People skills
Balance work/personal	Flexible	Positive
Change agent	Goal Oriented	Problem solver
Cheerleader	Humble	Quality manager
Comfortable with challenges	Humorous	Reliable
	Inspiring	Respected
Compassionate	Integrity	Risk taker
Committed	Intelligent	Succession planner
Communicator	Keep your cool	Synergetic
Compromising	Loyal	Team oriented
Continuously improving	Maintain relationships	Understands organization
	Mentor	
Confident	Motivated	Trainer
Consistent	Nonjudgmental	Trusted
Courageous	Objective	Willing to relocate
Creative		Work ethic
Curious		

Balancing the Age Gap

The article entitled "Role Reversal," by Jane Hawkrigg, in the *Canadian HR Reporter*, March 2006, notes that when young managers join the leadership team, they often find themselves dealing with entrenched workers old enough to be their parents. Savvy organizations recognize the challenges an emerging leader faces when it comes to supervising and encouraging associates from a different generation. An experienced coach, aware of the specific challenges these emerging leaders face, will suggest:

1. Put the leader in the worker's shoes.

2. Don't allow the new leader to stereotype the associates.

3. Make sure that the new team shares their experiences and insights with the new leader.

4. Make certain the new leader realizes there could be fear and resentment on the part of the associates. And, what can the new leader do to support associates' learning and growth?

5. Make certain the leader knows how the associates get their work done.

6. Direct the new leader to meet one-on-one with more seasoned associates to build rapport.

7. Hold regular feedback meetings with more seasoned associates.

8. Enlist associates who deliver on the vision.

NETWORKING

Emerging leaders learn early in their careers how to be plugged into a network. This is how they will get noticed as a supervisor and manager. Networking is often contrary to our desire to be a humble person. It requires a sense of assertiveness. Here are some guidelines to follow when networking that have been authored by Mel Kaufman of *Professional Powers*:

1. Arrive early and choose who you will be meeting by reviewing the guest list the day before.

2. Networking is not selling; it is gathering information.

3. Always begin each communication exchange with a question.

4. Join at least one community organization.

5. If you go with another associate, split at the door.

6. It is network, not net "sit."

7. On your business card, your organization's name should be two times the size of your name.

8. Have an effective introductory statement prepared for each event.

9. Be a host, not a guest.

10. Avoid foursomes, threesomes are best.

11. Talk to as many people as possible by getting out of your comfort zone.

12. If a follow-up call is required, do so within twenty-four hours.

You are now ready to "lead yourself" through the management phase, on your way to becoming the leader you dream to be.

Lastly, some more advice from Colin Powell, who said: "If I have not been explicitly told 'yes,' I cannot do it, or if I have not been explicitly told 'no,' I can. The moral of the story becomes, do not ask, but be prudent, not reckless. Do not wait for the official blessing to try things out."

Chapter Eight

References

Anonymous. "The Class of 2001." *Management Review*, December 1999, 88 (11): 23–25.

Alsop, Ron. *The Trophy Kids Grow Up*. San Francisco: Jossey-Bass, 2008.

Deal, Jennifer. "Generational Differences." *Leadership Excellence*, 2007, 24 (6): 11.

Dries, Nicky, Ronald Pepermans, and Evelien De Kerpel. "Exploring Four Generations' Beliefs about Career." *Journal of Managerial Psychology*, 2008, 23 (8): 907–28.

Elmore, Tim. "*A Generation of Paradox*." The Leadership Link Growing Leaders, Inc. 2008. Retrieved on May 12, 2009, from www.growingleaders. com Web site: http://www.growingleaders.com/images/stories/a%20 generation%20of%20paradox.pdf

Harrari, Oren. *The Leadership Secrets of Colin Powell*. New York: McGraw Hill, 2002.

Hawkrigg, Jane. "Role Reversal." *Canadian HR Reporter*, March 2006, 19 (5): 13.

Mathews, Dan, Executive Vice President & Chief Operating Officer. National Automatic Merchandising Association. A Lecture to HB 451, December 3, 2007.

Prof. King, Dr. Cichy suggested to cite his name in the contents of chapter 8.

Ruch, Will. "Full Engagement." *Leadership Excellence*, December 2005, 22 (12): 11.

Trinka, Jim. "Great Leaders." *Leadership Excellence*, July 2005, 22 (7): 17.

Wood, John, and Tricia Vilkinas. "Characteristics Associated with Success: CEO's Perspectives." *Leadership & Organization Development Journal*, 2005, 26 (3): 186–96.

PART IV

LEADERSHIP: FINAL STEPS

Chapter Nine–
Managing Change

*"However good or bad a situation is, it will change.
And you should frame every so-called disaster with
these words: in five years will this really matter?"*

Chapter Ten–
Leadership Possibilities

*"Your job will not take care of you when you are sick.
Your family and friends will. So, stay in touch."*

Chapter Eleven–
Conclusion

*"Invest your energy in the positive present moment,
not on gossip, issues of the past, or things you cannot
control."*

Welcome to Your Leadership
Position

Chapter Nine
Managing Change

Leading Others

Now that we are aware of the importance of knowing others (feelings and emotions) and serving others, we must expand our knowledge of some of the finer points regarding leading others. This will include how to change an organization's culture, reviewing how to mentor the organization's human assets by challenging people, how to coach high performers, what competencies are needed to lead others, what characteristics must exist to be an effective leader, and what leadership possibilities exist for the future.

We must assume that you will have the opportunity to have an impact on your organization's culture, especially as you progress toward a leadership position. To be able to make improvements regarding flaws in the organization's culture or realize what culture requirements are missing, we are providing a list of ideal culture characteristics for your review and use in assessing your organization's status.

Accessible leadership	Input of associates used in planning
Assessment process in place	Integrity a priority
Associates know self	Keep it simple
Attract the best, brightest, and creative people	Listening expected
Barriers removed	Manage by walking around
Benchmarking practiced	Mission clear and alive
Career development	Nondiscriminatory
Changing organization	Orientation program important
Communication open	Ownership of processes/principals
Community support	Passionate leadership
Compensation competitive	Positive attitude
Cooperative culture	Process oriented
Customer focused	Professionalism at 100%
Dignified treatment of associates	Recognition
Diversity used as strength	Respect for everyone
Emotional intelligence	Risk taking encouraged
Entrepreneurial attitudes supported	Self-directed teams
Everyone involved	Servant leadership
Family orientation	Strategic thinking
Fiscal responsibility	Team first attitude
Fun in the workplace	Technically strong
Golden rule practice	Trust in leadership
Hands-on leadership	Values are the core
Incentives in place	Vision clear and alive
Information shared	

Leading Change

Inevitably as a manager, you will be able to interject or create your choices for culture change in your department. However, keep in mind that the change must not be counter to the wishes of leadership. For example, if leadership has made it clear that major policy/procedure changes must come from the top, it will not be wise to implement a change in procedure in your department that would isolate the department from others in the organization. But, you could make it clear to your associates that they have a voice and that suggestions for change are welcomed within their department.

While the leader is ultimately responsible for managing change in the organization, most recommendations for change are born within the teams of associates, particularly during the annual strategic planning process.

> At HDS Services, we adopted the planning model of the Michigan National Guard, which was the recipient of the State's Malcolm Baldrige Quality Award in 2004. Colonel Barry Meyers was the Guard's point person and consulted with our team. He guided us through the transition to a best-in-class planning process.
>
> He emphasized that the strategic plan could not be static or carved in stone but had to be dynamic in order to be effective because the environment is ever changing. This is driven by the company's and customer needs, changing markets, new technology, and new opportunities.

Most planning processes coincide with an organization's fiscal year so that the costs associated with the business plan are included in the annual financial plan. Development of the business plan is accomplished by the leadership team at a two- or three-day meeting. The first order of business is generally revisiting the organization's vision, mission, and values to make sure they are still linked to the organization's direction, and include feedback from all organizational levels. Then, there is a discussion of the environmental assessment, which includes customer needs, economics, equipment, facilities, information management, leadership/management changes, manpower, market trends and demographics, statutory change, and technology.

This is followed by a thorough SWOT (Strengths, Weaknesses, Opportunities, Threats) Analysis. The review includes all goals, objectives, and strategies, and presents metrics and timelines. The plan should be published and presented by the leaders and their immediate team.

As David Cottrell states in his book *Twelve Choices That Lead To Your Success*: "People who disagree with you are not necessarily your enemies, unless their disagreement centers on the values you are trying to uphold. Whatever the consequences, never sacrifice your values. But, be aware that by making the choice not to sacrifice your values, you will create enemies (people whose values, goals, and objectives are different than yours). So, ask the question: 'Who are my enemies?' The key to dealing with your enemies is being able to identify who they are and understand why they have chosen to be your enemy."

We encourage you to become a powerful manager who is confident and in control of their destiny. But make the right choices, especially if you may be challenging the system or the leadership of the organization.

FUN WHILE YOU WORK

You will note that one of the culture characteristics was putting fun in the workplace. The two most notable examples of organizations that stress fun in the workplace are the Pike Place Fish Market and the St. Paul Saints baseball organization. Both organizations stress the importance of living and teaching the organization's vision, while having fun.

The Saints are more service-excellence oriented, while the Pike Place Fish Market is based on creativity and getting involved with the customers. There are simply three key concepts in the Saints' success. First, the associates are encouraged to discover their passion. Mike Veeck, the Saints' president, described this concept as "the thing behind your eyes, that machine, is much more sophisticated than anything that we will build in several lifetimes. And then, it's governed by this thing called heart." When we are able to put our heart or passion in our everyday work, not only will we as an individual be noticed, but the success this approach brings to the organization is immense. Our enthusiasm will inspire others and eventually be a motivating factor throughout the organization.

Secondly, the Saints' management encourages all associates to bring a positive attitude to work. In addition to the previous discussions about having a positive attitude in chapter six, the Saints make it clear that positive attitude is every associate's choice and responsibility. Both positive and negative attitudes are contagious. If you have a poor attitude at home, you are more likely to bring it to work, and vice versa. Have you ever played golf with someone who complains after almost every stroke? Or, how many people do you know who phone you just to complain about their day? If you have experienced these situations, you know from experience how those people affect you through that brief experience and perhaps the entire day. With the Saints' culture there is a mentality that having a positive attitude is based on knowing the difference between taking your job seriously and not taking yourself too seriously. Again, as pointed out by David Cottrell in *Twelve Choices*: "Possessing a positive attitude is a choice we can make every day in both the workplace and in our personal lives." And the last concept deals with associates displaying to everyone—both peers and customers—that they care. In other words, the Saints treat their customers with respect, gratitude, and an intense sense of wanting to please. This also opens the door for more creativity and freedom to discuss options and other ways of doing business. It is really quite simple—just be nice to people.

THINKING POSITIVELY

Roz and Ben Zander believe that "Leadership is an Art of Possibility." Again, we are focusing on the positive side of leadership and imagining that there are no barriers or negative thoughts or images. They support that we should start all associates out with an A—in other words, a perfect score. This gives them possibilities to live into, rather than expectations to live up to. These associates tend to think more highly of themselves, which expands their limits of performance and creates more of an opportunity for success. If we have all been B-performers, that would be our normal expectation; but when given an A by leadership at the outset, we have a better chance or possibility of performing at a higher level because we know that the leaders believe in us. This tends to encourage us to also believe in ourselves, that we can deliver results at an A-level.

Encourage your associates not to complain about change, and conversely, to pursue the benefits of change. The power of the collective attitudes of associates will always outnumber the problems. Keep in mind that most people believe that a successful life is one of security. They neglect to realize that the only secure individual is one that that does not take any risks in the name of improvement. Complaining about change is not beneficial at all. In fact, it is like complaining that the salt is salty.

Make an effort to not seek security in the good old days, because they are never going to return. Most individuals who are insecure attempt to control as many aspects of the environment around them as possible. This mental effort to know everything will more than likely confuse your thinking and will lead you to operate with only the information at hand. You must realize that you cannot possibly know in advance what is going to happen. However, this should not prevent you from thinking strategically and planning for the future by being a forward thinker. Also, it is beneficial to call on friends, family, associate team members, and the community in order to constantly connect with others whose perceptions can generate security by informing you about their thoughts. With this knowledge you will possess a new sense of meaning and will be better prepared to connect with the world around you. When you find this new purpose, you will feel more confident and significant. Confidence will lead to positive thinking.

The leader must also emulate a "can-do" attitude, which enlivens the associates and immediately removes barriers that hinder performance. Elizabeth Edersheim, in her article about management sage Peter Drucker's *Unfinished Chapter: The Role of the CEO*, reflects about "Drucker's definition of an effective manager as one who achieves results. This is contrary to the traditional definition of a manager as somebody who has subordinates. Most organizations staff their problems and starve their opportunities. When people start talking about their problems, I say, 'No wait a minute. Let's first look at the opportunities.' I try to make them look forward rather than backward."

It goes beyond positive attitude because the leader literally looks the associates in the eyes and encourages their potential to do better. Suddenly there is this passion in the associates, and the relationship between leadership and the team is alive, strong, and positive. The voices in the associates' heads are totally positive.

IMPORTANCE OF MENTORING

This leads us once again to the mentoring process, how it is done, and the rules for following through. Successful leaders find that working as a mentor with emerging leaders gives both an experience that is very energizing, even fun. It is because they take this responsibility to a more personal level. Robert Gondossy and Lauren Contlon, in their article "The little things that develop great leadership," report that some of IBM's best mentors work with over thirty people above and beyond their direct reports. They believe that it is a plus to move people and a minus to hoard them. The lesson learned is to never hold on to a great person with strong potential for leadership. Other candidates will notice your results and passion and select you as their next mentor.

Effective leaders and the best managers realize that mentoring is about giving, sharing the concerns of their mentoring partner, and using their character as a model. The giving process takes patience and a long-term commitment because results do not appear overnight. The mentor has to work through the various stages of the process to gain trust, share experiences, discover others, plan, and prioritize action steps. The strength of the relationship between the mentor and the partner must be based on character in order to build trust and create openness and discussions. The plan must be shared with the partner and include a clear, step-by-step process and the destination which is mutually developed. To effectively mentor the partner, both first must get to know each other extremely well. The more the mentor knows about what motivates the partner and the partner's personal values, vision, and mission, the more successful the relationship will become. The leaders who are the most respected are those who are the most effective mentors.

In the mentoring process, it is best to work with the partner on improving the partner's strengths, because devoting time to weaknesses will not provide quick growth. Take advantage of the partner's natural talents. Also, as a mentor, you can suggest, but do not make choices for the partner, both professionally and personally.

FIVE LEADERSHIP COMPETENCIES

There are five broad sets of competencies that are common among the best leaders who lead change. They are character, credibility, interpersonal skills, being results focused, and the ability to lead organizational change.

Character is at the core of effective leadership. This includes being open and available to all associates in setting the example for those who work with you. This makes you authentic, which creates the standards of honesty and integrity. To demonstrate impeccable character in a leadership role, you must always practice ethics in dealing with issues, do what you say, do the right things, lead by example, and follow through on your commitments.

Credibility is earned over time through the use of expertise and technical skills. As you progress as a manager, you must gain these skills as fast and effectively as possible. You maintain your credibility by staying up-to-date in your field of expertise, understanding the details that support skills, sharing your opinions and knowledge with your team, asking the right questions when troubleshooting, and being innovative in promoting change.

Interpersonal skills are the ways you interact with others. Interpersonal skills are used in solving problems, mentoring, and analyzing issues. Once the problem is defined, determine the root causes and intervene with action. Then follow up to determine if the results are in line with expectations. Remember to constantly seek feedback and never end the process of developing yourself through learning. Your management team will be looking for you to bring the latest and best leadership practices to the organization. Learn from your failures and never shy away from risk, because this is the root of reward.

This brings us to the mandate of being focused on results. It blends in with being a change maker. Change and results come from goal setting and strategic thinking. You and your team will strategize for improvement and thus set improvement goals and objectives to achieve the goals. As a leader you must be committed to these goals and expect accountability from your team. If they lose interest as time passes, goals are not met, then you will have failed as a leader. So make sure the goals are measurable in order to promote the principles of continuous improvement. Recall that SMART goals are Specific, Measurable, Attainable, Realistically high, and Timely.

Everyone knows that organizations must change on a continuous basis in order to improve and stay in front of the competition by answering the needs and expectations of evolving markets and customers. But leading change is a challenge to many managers and leaders. It requires strategic and forward thinking and a strong sense of what is best for the organization in the long run. One of the most challenging components of change management is aligning the team and its members with the values, vision, mission, and strategic plan. This requires open and frequent communication, well-thought-out training, and mentoring. In a nutshell, the leader becomes the champion of the transformation from the old to the new. When the work environment is open and receptive to ideas, there is less challenge, and members of the teams step forward to become more responsible and accountable.

The leader must have a team of executives who form a change integration team. This is the team that consolidates independent and interdependent projects within the organization. Integration efforts will help to avoid any resistance to change. Most resistance surfaces in the form of political maneuvering or totally ignoring the change and hoping it will go away. People will align with the changes only when they agree with the need to change the process. So, individuals need to understand early on in the process the reasons why change is a good thing.

One of Colin Powell's leadership lesson states: "The commander in the field is always right and the rear echelon wrong unless proven otherwise." This is excellent advice for leaders who are involved in making decisions concerning changing their organization. The associates and the management teams in the field are the best resources of ideas concerning change. They create and deliver and evaluate the organization's products and services and experiences every day. The effective leader knows where to go for advice regarding the crucial decisions.

CHAPTER NINE

REFERENCES

Cantlon, Lauren, and Robert Gondossy. "The Little Things That Develop Great Leadership." *Leader to Leader,* summer 2003, 29:54–61.

Cottrell, David. *12 Choices That Lead to Your Success.* Dallas: Cornerstone Leadership Institute, 2005.

Edersheim, Elizabeth. "Peter Drucker's Unfinished Chapter." *Leader to Leader,* summer 2007, 2007 (45): 40.

Harari, Oren. *The Leadership Secrets of Colin Powell.* New York: McGraw Hill, 2002.

Veeck, Mike. *Fun is Good.* Emmaus, PA: Rodale Press, 2005, and CRM Learning.

Zender, Ben, and Roz Zender, "Leadership: An Art of Possibility", American Media, Groh Publications, Inc., 2000

CHAPTER TEN
LEADERSHIP POSSIBILITIES

LEADERSHIP POSSIBILITIES

As you progress through the various management positions in your leadership journey, the duties you perform and responsibilities you have will change. How you adjust to these progressively changing duties and responsibilities will determine your next steps for leadership advancement in the future. Is the leader of the organization ready to move you? Does the leader give you clear communication concerning present performance, personal mentoring progress, and readiness for the next position? Do you discuss future leadership possibilities with your leader? If the answers are yes, do you feel positive about the discussions? Are you sure the leader is sincere? What does the leader's leader think about you? Is there a positive relationship? Remember that the higher up in the organization this leader is, the more milestones are used to measure progress. In other words, managers tend to measure progress in smaller increments because they work with the details every day. This is not the case with leaders who work with milestones.

The "Leadership Lesson from the Eagle" is: "Life is not measured by the number of breaths you take. It is measured by the number of moments that take your breath away."

BUILDING A TEAM

There is one leadership skill we have yet to discuss, and that is building a team. As a manager you built your team through associate selection, proper orientation, associate skills/competencies development, empowerment, recognition, and mentoring. This has now changed to a greater focus on strategic planning, implementation, and managing change. In other words, you have progressed in the leadership model as part of your leadership journey. Believe it or not, the same qualities, secrets, and keys exist in the management and leadership team models. The primary differences found in the people you have on your team are their expectations, their personal needs, and how they relate with their peers and you. There are no boundaries that limit what a leadership team can accomplish. Each change that they work together to implement has an enormous impact on the entire organization and expands the leadership possibilities.

There are those periods of time in the history of all organizations that the issues facing leadership are such that the impending outcome could lead to disaster on one side and a successful milestone on the other. These are the challenges that require team input and full discussion. Even though the ultimate decision will be made by the leader, he or she must have the full range of input from the team. Also, there must be consensus among the team, and the leader must announce his or her agreement at the meeting before moving forward. Thus, there is total closure to the input and planning phase of dealing with challenges. Now it is time to take action and reinforce confidence in the organization's leadership. Remember that your team is going to be diverse in its makeup, so there is additional cause for developing common objectives.

A HISTORICAL STORY OF LEADERSHIP

One of the most appropriate stories about leadership and what can be accomplished goes back to the early 1800s. Jack Aldrich's article "Leading into the Unknown; How Lewis and Clark Built a Great Team," recalls the challenges facing the Corps of Discovery and the success of the entire team under the leadership of explorers Lewis and Clark.

Members of the Lewis and Clark team had a deep respect for each of their team members and treated them with the utmost support and courtesy. Lewis and Clark were unafraid to pitch in and take a hands-on approach to managing the expedition to travel the Mississippi, Missouri, and Columbia rivers from St. Louis to the Pacific Ocean.

Their team was made up of Native Americans and people from France, with each person possessing unique talents. The leaders taught each team member to rely less on their own talents and more on the contributions of other members. They also encouraged flexibility and initiative. They encountered unprecedented challenges, such as portaging the rivers, crossing mountain ranges, riding unknown rapids, and surviving the winter in the northern plains. The leaders would not let them quit and made sure the team was confident of achieving almost anything. For the return trip, Lewis and

Clark subdivided the team into smaller teams and empowered them to be on their own. Everyone made it through the return trip, and the two-year adventure continues to be pointed to as a leadership model. The "Leadership Lesson from the Eagle" here is: "Give your associates the freedom to grow, and remember that great achievements involve higher levels of risk."

MENTORING OTHERS

As you approach the bridge to a leadership position, you should evaluate what you have done regarding mentoring your management replacement. You can never start the mentoring process too soon because you can expect your leader to inquire about who you would choose to take your place. This will more than likely be a subject discussed by the two of you during your final year in the management ranks. Again, you will have been mentoring managers over the years, but your mentoring goals and strategies will be very narrowly focused during this final year.

You will learn very quickly that leaders frequently devote more of their time to the challenges the organization will face in the future. In other words, they attempt to identify areas of uncertainty and the leadership possibilities. By doing this, and preparing leadership and the management teams for these challenges, the organization gains a competitive advantage.

In another historic leader presentation, one of our students chose the *Last Lecture* and Professor Randy Pausch as her leader. Randy was asked to give a last lecture. In his situation, he did not need to pretend it was his last chance to speak, since he had recently been diagnosed with terminal cancer with only months to live. Randy chose to put together a speech that was not about death, but instead was about life. He stressed the importance of overcoming obstacles: "… brick walls are there for a reason: they let us prove how badly we really want things." He explained how exciting it is to enable the dreams of others. And, as you get older you will find that enabling the dreams of others is even more fun. Also, he reminded everyone of the significance of achieving their own dreams and seizing every moment, because time is all you have, and you may find one day that you have less than you think.

Possibilities and uncertainties are identified by teams, because no leader has all the answers. There is nothing wrong with leaders demonstrating vulnerability and the fact that they do not have all of the answers. So, engage your team in looking at the future possibilities and feeling empowered to share concerns and ideas. This leads to team members having knowledge of what the future will bring, rather than worrying about what they do not know.

A "Leadership Lesson from the Eagle" tells us: "Leaders are passionate about what they do; believe, and know that one person can often make the difference. But, also recognize that the tough decisions often require comprehensive team input."

In Jona Madsen's article "How to be a Better Boss," he lists ten measures of effective managers. We have already discussed eight of these, which include accessibility, associate relationships, recognition, empowerment, communication, vision and the ability to rally associates, leading by example, and ethical behavior. A ninth measure involves customizing leadership's approach for each individual associate. It is one thing to know self and others. But it is another to develop customized relationships with each associate. This is contrary to the adage that all associates should be treated equally. All associates are different, and, in order to maximize your leadership effectiveness, you must vary your approach to mentoring each one. Some will need more direction than others. Some will need more recognition than others (remember the self-esteem examples).

Addressing Poor Performance

The tenth measure is the ability to address poor performance. If you recognize and understand the linkage between poor performance, lost customers, and organization downsizing in reaction to lost business, you will not experience difficulty in being honest with poorly performing associates. One of the responsibilities of the leader is to confront the brutal facts and connect others to the reality as it exists. This helps them see the real leadership possibilities. Underperformers either do not have the resources, including skills and capabilities, to succeed or do not have the desire. You can coach these underperformers and turn the situation around, but it takes a strong evaluative process and a strong desire to see your associates succeed. In short, you have the responsibility to help them see the possibilities.

Balancing Family and Career

You will need to stress to your associates that family comes first, even though it will be the rare occasion that the two will clash head-on in your career. There is a correlation between being an effective leader and having a happy and fulfilling personal life. As you move along in your leadership journey, never lose sight of your dreams as a younger person. Those dreams revolve around family. When you looked in the mirror you saw a family situation, that was positive. So, do not allow those in your professional world to make decisions for you that relate to your personal life. Take control of your personal destiny, because the leader with strong personal relationships will always be more effective. All good leaders have a strong support system in their family and friends.

We have already introduced how effective leaders manage change by starting with the "ending" phase of current processes, to what is termed the "neutral" phase, and on to the "beginning" phase where the changes are implemented. Most changes are born in the strategic planning process. These plans are responsive to the organization's needs due to changing opportunities, new technology, and, most frequently, due to changing markets. The strategic culture of any organization is ever changing, so plans must be adaptable and should be based on flexibility.

The formal planning review should take place on an annual basis, according to Col. Barry Meyers, the quality champion at the Michigan National Guard. Their planning model was adopted at HDS Services and proved to be very successful. The HDS leadership team conducted a series of meetings which included the following steps:

1. Visit or revisit the vision, mission, and values

   a. Any revisions?

   b. Associate feedback?

   c. External forces—change necessary?

   d. Align with corporate journey

2. Quick discussion of company status

   a. External forces

   b. Market trends and demographics

   c. Economic factors

   d. Technology impact—information management

   e. Customer changes

   f. Regulatory changes

   g. Management/leadership changes

   h. Facilities review

   i. Personnel/development issues

   j. Equipment/distribution changes

3. SWOT analysis

    a. Strengths

    b. Weaknesses

    c. Opportunities

    d. Threats

4. Review goals, objectives, and strategies

    a. Delete accomplished objectives

    b. Develop new additions (use SMART goals model)

        • Specific

        • Measurable

        • Achievable

        • Reasonably high and Results oriented

        • Time defined

5. Review metrics

6. Review timeline for success

7. Publish plan

    a. Present to associates

    b. CEO involved in presentations and communication

    c. Formalized commitment

The plan should be folded into the organization's Balanced Scorecard, which mirrors the scorecard you completed earlier on in this book. It highlights all outcome areas and uses metrics to determine the baseline assessment of each outcome area, the targeted objectives and goals, and the current status, which would typically be documented on a quarterly basis. The scorecard also includes information regarding completion timelines.

You will know you have "arrived" at your leadership position when your leader informs you about the well-deserved promotion, or when the new leader imparts this information. So now what?

Basically, the same series of events that took place when you were assigned your first management position apply. Take your time. Meet with your new team, both in a group and individually. Demonstrate your communication skills and your values. Talk about your personal goals. Show respect and your willingness to be a coach and to be coached. Build your team and make sure all associates are in the most appropriate positions that mirror their strengths.

Now that you have arrived, you will have a much better idea of the components of the leadership career progression model. The positions include general manager, multiunit manager, organization officer, and CEO.

RESPONSIBILITIES OF THE LEADER

1. Strategic planning
   a. Participate at property level
   b. Manage at multiunit/officer levels
   c. Author, commit, and present plan at the CEO level
   d. Present to the shareholders
   e. Present planned proponents to community leaders

2. Financial planning
   a. Involved at the property level
   b. Manage at multiunit/officer level
   c. Coordinate, commit, and present plan to the team, board, and shareholders at the CEO level
   d. If publicly held, work with the SEC

3. Monitor performance
   a. Closely monitor financial, operational, and sales/marketing performance at property level
   b. Coordinate the efforts of the executive team in performance monitoring and change implementation at the office and CEO levels

4. Develop leadership team
   a. At all levels of leadership
   b. In every part of the organization
   c. Help all see the leadership possibilities

5. Public/community relations
   a. Involved at all levels of leadership
   b. Focused on the public/community

6. Relations with board of directors

    a. Coordinate board member involvement as CEO

    b. Coordinate board member selection

    c. Chair board meetings

7. Attend finance committee meetings

    a. Relations with financial institutions

    b. Involved with property expansion

These responsibilities may seem to be out of contact with associates, but the CEO can take a hands-on approach to the job by working very closely with members of the leadership team. The CEO must also be present at many property management meetings and recognition events. Remember that the members of your leadership team are the organization's stars, and stars are the best caretakers of customers. These same stars are also your best sales professionals. It is the stars who are not only responsible for the CEO's success, but in most cases are directly involved with the organization's success or failure. So, take good care of your organization's leadership human capital.

There is a striking correlation between great strategies and strong leaders, according to Michael Potter in his article "Leadership Excellence." Strategy is all about being different and positioning the organization, its products, and services to be unique in the industry.

Somewhere along the line of planning, someone will creatively define a new activity that no other organization is doing. The leader's responsibility is not to invent strategy but to provide the discipline to sustain a new position. When all the ideas come in from associates, customers, and suppliers, they should be considered for inclusion in the strategic plan as a creative twist or option without changing the direction of the strategies. This effort to include everyone in the process will lead to effective execution of the plan, because they will know exactly what to do in the decision-making process. Michael Potter goes on to say that there are three key principles that underlie strategic positioning:

*   Create a fit among all the organization's activities

*   Strategize about what not to do

*   Serve the needs of all customers in your market area.

We have chosen to close this chapter with some comments about applying your leadership qualities, keys, and secrets to your personal life. Jay Lorsch and Thomas Tierney covered this topic very well in an article entitled "Build the Life, not a Resume." Most managers expect to make sacrifices and work hard. And, the bonuses are great. But is this what they really want to do for the rest of their lives? Over time they want to make some trade-offs, to invest in family, the community, and personal passions. Many managers lose sight of what they once considered a priority in their life, that is, to maintain a balance between work and personal life. As a leader, you must stress this balance with your team and practice it yourself. Sometimes, fear of failure at work can create an unbalanced situation. This is when the leader must step in and remind the team members of the importance of engaging themselves in the lives of their family. In order to get to become an authentic, effective leader, family values must be a priority, and your commitment to uphold these with the team will enhance the success of the organization. This commitment becomes a strategic advantage for the organization, both in the associate selection process and retention.

Now that you have arrived and are officially a leader, do not forget how you got there. Continue to use and develop the principles and values that got you where you are today. You will not use them as much for your own success, but more so to promote the growth of your organization as a market leader. These truly reveal the leadership possibilities.

Your decisions as a leader will impact the organization much more than they did when you were a manager. So, be very deliberate in the decision-making process and involve your team so you have as much input and information as possible. Prioritize your work each day, and delegate as many challenges and projects as you comfortably can. The challenges that cause leaders the most trouble are those that create the most worry, because they are continually on the leader's mind and can create barriers to making good decisions.

Keep your mind clear and free of worrisome issues. Do not procrastinate; handle each piece of paper but once; do things now; stay in good physical condition; wake up alert; maintain the ongoing to-do list; handle e-mail/ paperwork immediately; eliminate clutter; make the most of meetings and do not tie up your associates in meetings that do not involve all participants; eat a light lunch; plan the next day before you go home; avoid working at home as much as possible; and manage your family involvement in order to not carry family issues to work the next day.

Your values are now alive and are like rocks you can depend on for strength. Achieve your goals; get your people involved, tell the team your expectations, and get out of their way. Respect your associates' needs; do not be judgmental. Challenge yourself, because self-esteem depends on it. Catch associates doing something right and cheer on the progress and share this with everyone. If you want associates to trust you, you will have to trust them first. Make sure your team members feel safe when giving feedback. Know your opponents but do not worry about them. These are just a few gems of advice that helped us become more effective leaders.

You know who you are today, and you know where you stand in your leadership journey. The question is whether you know how far you have to go before you are in a leadership position. The only given here is that you will be a totally different person when you become a leader. So, what will those differences be? If we can describe and identify these differences, it will make the transition easier to achieve. Unfortunately, you cannot look into the future and clearly identify the differences. But, what you can do is develop some managerial habits that will expedite the changes you achieve in making the transition. In addition to these practices, just ask yourself what you need to do to change and achieve your goals.

First and foremost, **be a Change Maker**. Be assertive and learn as much as you can about effectively managing your organization, and particularly about leading your team of people. Much of this will come from the **Mentor** that you selected, but some will also come from reading, seminars, and looking outside your organization for ideas (**Benchmarking**).

Be a **Networker.** Get to know as many people in your organization as possible. Attend all meetings and social events when invited. And, get involved in your organization's planning process.

Take on **Added Responsibilities.** You will meet many new people and gain an enormous amount of experience by volunteering. This will help you think more strategically because you will be exposed to different methods and processes.

CHAPTER TEN

REFERENCES

Karakas, Fahri. "A Portrait of the Leader in the Twenty-First Century." *Leadership in Action,* January/February 2007, 26 (6): 23.

Madsen, Jona. "How to be a Better Boss." *Buildings,* August 2005.

Meyers, Berry. "Strategic Planning General Review Cycle." 2003.

Pausch, Randy. *Last Lecture.*

Potter, Michael. *Leadership Excellence.* Provo 2006. 23: 6–7.

Tierney, Thomas, Jay Lorsch. "Build a Life Not a Resume." *Consulting to Management,* September 2002.

Uldrich, Jack. "Leading into the Unknown: How Lewis and Clark Built a Great Team." *Leader to Leader,* summer 2004.

CHAPTER ELEVEN
CONCLUSION

YOUR NEXT STEPS

As you now know, there are many steps in the leadership journey from student/ associate to supervisor to manager to leader. You should now have a clear understanding of how to be an effective manager and leader. Remember, this understanding is and will always be based on the expectations of your internal and external customers. You will learn through experience as an associate how to be an effective supervisor, as a supervisor how to be an effective manager, and as a manager how to be an effective leader. This requires time, but hopefully you now understand how to make this transition much faster than others.

What do you think the most important trait is for a manager or leader to be successful? In a recent article, four managers were interviewed, and the results were not surprising. The traits mentioned include communication, approachability, integrity, and enthusiasm. Associates will respond more openly to a manager that is a good communicator and is enthusiastic about the organization and their role in the organization. Integrity is the one trait that is a "must-have." No manager or leader can be successful without it, because associates will not respect the aspiring leader. Integrity has components of honesty, openness, approachability, trust, creativity, credibility, partnership, and a culture of empowerment. Will the organization that you eventually lead mirror the part of the organization that you now or will manage? We hope so! If it does, you understand and practice the qualities, keys, and secrets outlined in this book.

Your leadership traits will be an outgrowth of your management skills and will attest to the golden rule of leading others as you want to be led yourself. You and your associates will want their organization's biggest asset to be the people and will behave to make that the reality.

There are some key differences between management and leadership that sometimes create problems for recently promoted leaders. The most prevalent pitfall is that as a manager you may achieve results individually, and as a leader you must get results by listening to and working with teams. So, as you are promoted from supervision to management to leadership, do not believe someone who advises you to keep doing what you have been doing. Another pitfall is the fact that many organizations are cutting back their workforce, thus there are fewer layers of supervision and management. In the past you may have been responsible for managing half the number of associates that are presently in that department. This is an adjustment of 100 percent.

As a supervisor or manager, you will have to decide how soon you want to become a leader. You can be cautious and more methodical, but this would probably lead to a possible leadership promotion in fifteen years. Or, you can decide to be more assertive and strategically network to be considered for leadership promotion in less than ten years. We would hope you would choose the latter option. We were successful at achieving this shorter-term goal, and, as outlined in chapter one, *you **can** do it.* So, you can use the suggestions in this book and achieve your goal in the next ten years. Here are some pointers to further assist you with your leadership journey.

First, remember that you can mirror what Rob and others achieved by becoming a leader after spending less than ten years in management. His attributes included having a clear vision (knowing what you want and where you are going), being passionate about your management position (sales, in Rob's case), continually networking to be known to the organization's leadership, possessing a customer-first attitude, and being an effective communicator. In other words, you can duplicate what Rob achieved by knowing what you want and possessing a sense of destiny, loving your position and organization, being noticed, taking care of the customers, and relating well with associates, customers, and peers. Sounds simple, and it really is. This reminds us to encourage you to know and practice the value of keeping everything in simple form. Too much information only clutters the communication process.

Effective managers concentrate on process flow rather than finding fault with their people. Remember that 85 percent of your challenges will come in the form of challenges with process management, not people management.

Your integrity will be challenged more than once in your career. It happens to most supervisors, managers, and leaders. The key to being able to avoid any temptation is being prepared for the challenge. By being prepared, we mean that your appropriate response will come naturally and without question. You achieve this level of resolve by thinking through the risks and applying your values. As a leader you will personally investigate your organization's internal processes, barriers to effective process management, systems, communication methodology, and culture. Remember, pressure will eventually show up to test your leadership.

Get to know what your associates think of you as a supervisor, manager, and leader. The evaluation process must involve the associates' review of your performance. The reframing exercise in getting to know your inner world frames the importance of continuously improving.

The most important question to ask attendees at strategic meetings is: "What can our team or organization do to give us a strategic advantage?" We will guarantee you will get immediate and worthwhile feedback. Continually dehassle your organization with the input of associates by using great questions that involve customers and the organization's key indicators, such as satisfaction, retention, and recruiting quality candidates.

We discussed the decision-making process (managing change) that works all the time, but we did not present it graphically. So, here it is again in another format.

Obtain Feedback (ideas and issues) From
Associates
External Customers
Peers
Leadership
Stakeholders
Suppliers
Community
"Get Everyone Involved"

Conduct Root Cause Analysis
"Focus on Cause, Not Symptoms"

PDCA
PLAN—Determine Interventions
DO—Take Action
CHECK—Measure Results
ACT—If It Works, Make It Standard Procedure
"Decisions to Act Require Courage, Creativity, and Risk"

Many interventions for change will surface at any given time. This requires leadership's coordination and making certain that the changes are integrated, because separate teams with separate charters can create confusion. Leaders must communicate with everyone so they know how they strategically fit together.

Values are meant to be maintained throughout your career. Do not lose them or water them down. The most important pertain to integrity, courage, character, and trust. Many people have asked us how we were successful in raising our children. Our answer has not changed since we first responded many years ago. Successful parents have faith in their children to survive their young years, because the children experience a learning situation, mostly on their own, but sometimes from their parents. They also learn (both good and bad) from their peers. Selecting the right friends is important here. Leaders, like parents, must be resilient in order to survive crises, failure, and everyday challenges. Share your values with associates, children, and those you mentor.

There is a deeper purpose in life than being a successful manager or leader. "Great achievements are only reached by those who dared believe that something inside them was superior to circumstance" (Anonymous). In other words, achievements do not just happen.

Leaders are held accountable by stakeholders, board members, customers, and, most importantly, by associates. So, do not forget to align yourself with customers and associates. And always follow through on your commitments to others. Never forget what you have promised to do. Keep a written list of commitments and work diligently to keep the list short.

In Fahri Karakas's article in the *Reader Forum*, January/February 2007, "A Portrait of the Leader in the Twenty-First Century," he tends to agree with Tim Elmore's views previously presented about the shortage of good leaders today. He states that everyone is hungry today for a new paradigm of leadership. Today's leaders have to deal with a totally new set of challenges, including globalization, uncertainty brought on by terrorism, global warming, cultural intermingling, corporate scandal, and chaotic complexities. He believes the mind-sets and heart-sets required by leaders in the twenty-first century for the most part are generally similar to some of those in the past. These include passion, creativity, meaning, wisdom, vision, courage, and integrity. However, he also mentions consciousness, insight, openness, intuition, flexibility, accountability, authenticity, care, and nurturing. This latter group of leadership attributes is comprised of the essential skills that have been lost over time or put aside by others. Our opinion is that they disappeared because of the fast-paced, chaotic, technology-driven business environment we are working in today.

You will not only learn and develop yourself from contact with leadership; most of your development will result from contact with associates. So, listen to them and understand generational differences. These associates will help you be successful. Sometimes being responsible means making associates angry. The flip side is that treating all associates equally and wanting everyone to like you only leads to mediocrity. When this happens, the only associates that end up angry are the good ones. And most will not be happy when you leave them to take your leadership position. So be prepared to return in the future to visit and thank them.

Chapter Eleven

References

Karakas, Fahri. "A Portrait of the Leader in the Twenty-First Century." *LIA*, 26 (6).

CHAPTER TWELVE
YOUR EMERGING LEADERSHIP JOURNEY PLAN

Your Emerging Leadership Journey Plan is your plan, not anyone else's plan. While others may give you input and provide guidance as mentors, when it comes right down to it, you are the owner of your plan. As the sole proprietor of your plan, it is your responsibility to design and author it, and then put the plan into action. This concluding chapter presents an outline for Your Emerging Leadership Plan. It is a starting point, because you will want to tailor and customize it to your unique emerging leadership journey. We wish you peace and success in your emerging leadership journey.

My Emerging Leadership Journey Plan

Today's Date   _____

Date in Five Years   _____

This Emerging Leadership Journey Plan is for you to use for the next five years. Reflect and write where your personal leadership journey will take you in the next five years. Be as specific as you can, because being specific will help you focus on those elements of your plan that will help you the most in your journey.

- Clearly state your personal values, vision, and mission.
My values (how I intend to act/behave) are:

_____
_____
_____

- My vision (what I want to create) is:

_____

_____

_____

- My mission (my purpose in life) is:

_____

_____

_____

- Describe how credibility fits into your foundation for leadership.

_____

_____

_____

- Apply the leadership framework to your personal leadership journey by describing how you intend to practice each of the following:

  - Know self

_____

_____

_____

  - Know self/lead self

_____

_____

_____

  - Know others

_____

_____

_____

  - Know others/lead others

_____

_____

_____

- Lead change

_____

_____

_____

- What you will apply—be specific—to your personal leadership journey from the following:
  - Myers-Briggs Type Indicator assessment

_____

_____

  - Emotional Intelligence assessment

_____

_____

  - Managing your career progression

_____

_____

  - Leadership qualities, keys, secrets, and essentials

_____

_____

  - Integrity

_____

_____

  - Servant leadership

_____

_____

- Leadership Lessons from the Eagle

_____

_____

_____

- Leaders you have known and admired

_____

_____

_____

- Describe where your personal leadership journey will take you in the next 5 years—describe **details** for **each** year: year 1, year 2, year 3, year 4, and year 5. For **each** year, write answers to the following:

  - How will you know it?

_____

_____

_____

  - What will be happening?

_____

_____

_____

  - How will it manifest itself?

_____

_____

_____

  - What will be the outcomes? Desired results?

_____

_____

_____

Describe at least three ways that you will continuously improve as you move on in your personal leadership journey.

_____

_____

_____

Include a summary about where you intend to go in your emerging leadership journey.

_____

_____

_____

The more details that you provide in this assessment, the better you will be able to help yourself continue to progress in your personal leadership journey.

Sources of Epitaphs

1. "No one is in charge of your happiness, attitude, or career except you."
   http://nashvillenaiw.org/Documents/May_08Newsletter.pdf

2. "Make peace with your past so it will not spoil the present."
   http://www.freedomsphoenix.com/Feature-Article.htm?Info=0056694

3. "Do not take yourself so seriously, because no one else does. And, what other people think of you is none of your business."
   http://www.livingplenty.com/content/50-life-quotes

4. "If you tell the truth, you do not have to remember anything."—Mark Twain
   http://www.jdcjr.us/Quotes3.html

5. "Life is too short to waste time hating anyone."
   http://www.minorityprofessionalnetwork.com/contentdata.asp?id=9756

6. "Remember that you are too blessed to be stressed."
   http://www.minorityprofessionalnetwork.com/contentdata.asp?id=9756

7. "You don't have to win every argument. Agree to disagree."
   http://www.answerology.com/index.aspx?template=blog_this.ascx&question_id=2669294

8. "You cannot get swept off your feet if you are sitting down."
   www.quotegarden.com/wise-words.html

9. "Stand up and be noticed."—Claire Camden
   www.4mat.com/news/**stand-up-and-be-noticed**-spotlight-on-cbsbutler-s-new-website-news-99331234472

10. "Do not compare your life to others. You have no idea what their journey is all about."
www.blogged.com/about/**life**-tips-**journey**/

11. "However good or bad a situation is, it will change. And you should frame every so-called disaster with these words: in five years will this really matter?"
www.cha**bad**.org/blogs/blog_cdo/aid/833271/jewish/Twenty-**five**-Wise-Principles.htm

12. "Your job won't take care of you when you are sick. Your family and friends will. So, stay in touch."
www.**care**pages.com/blogs/wecarryeachother/posts/some-inspiration

13. "Invest your energy in the positive present moment, not on gossip, issues of the past, or things you cannot control."
http://www.citehr.com/140928-check-out-handbook-2009-really-useful.html

INDEX

9182044R0

Made in the USA
Lexington, KY
06 April 2011